Elementary English for the restaurant industry

Ready to Order

Ronalda Puritch
Randall Bryers
CELTA Tutors

Anne Baude
Montserrat Iglesias
Anna Iñesta

Longman
www.longman.com

Students' Book

Pearson Education Limited
Edinburgh Gate
Harlow
Essex CM20 2JE
England and Associated Companies throughout the world.

www.longman.com

First published 2002

ISBN 0 582 429552

Set in Trade Gothic 10pt / 13pt.

Printed in Spain by Graficas Estella.

Acknowledgements

We are grateful to the following for permission to reproduce copyright photographs:

Art Directors and TRIP for 47 bottom, 50 bottom and 79 (1), (2), (3), (5), (7) and 79 (8); Anthony Blake Photo Library for 12 bottom left. 47 top and 50 top; Cephas for 29, 54 left and 54 right; Corbis Images for 59 middle and 89 left; DK Images for 25 (all), 79 (4) and 89 right; Empics for 79 (6); Greg Evans International for 54 middle; Getty One Stone for 59 left; Image State for 59 right; IPC Pictures for 55; Rex Features for 12 bottom right, 57 (all) and Rye Tourist office for 33.

The cover photographs were kindly supplied by Anthony Blake Photo Library (top left), Cephas (bottom) and Britstock IFA (top right).

All other photos not acknowledged are © Pearson Education/Trevor Clifford.

Freelance Picture Research by Jacqui Rivers.

Illustrated by Mark Watkinson, William Donohoe and Jane Spencer.

Designed by Wendy Birch.

The authors wish to thank all their families and friends for their support.

The publishers and authors are very grateful to the following people and institutions for piloting and/or reporting on the manuscript:

Leila Belaid, Lyceé St Joseph, Chateau-Thierry, France; Anna Campaña, Marta Cànaves and Graham Stanley, Sant Ignasi-Sarrià, Escola Superior d'Hosteleria i Turisme, Barcelona, Spain; Antonio Cereceda, ESH Turismo, Madrid, Spain; Rosemary Habeeb-Richey, Munich, Germany; Toni Kelly, IES Bisbe Sivilla, Calella, Spain; Noreen Noonan, CRET, Briançon, France; Joanna Szerszunowicz, Studium Hotelarstwa i Obsługi Turystyki, Białystok, Poland.

Introduction

Ready to Order is for vocational students training to become chefs, bartenders and waiters. It is also suitable for professionals who wish to brush up their English. It caters for students from elementary to pre-intermediate level by providing activities for mixed ability groups.

Ready to Order consists of a coursebook, a workbook and a teacher's book. There is also a cassette / CD with all the model dialogues used in the coursebook.

The coursebook is set in a London restaurant called the Casablanca, which is part of the Hollywood Hotel. The book follows the daily lives of three main characters: Rosa (a cook), Jan (a waiter) and Peter (a bartender).

Ready to Order contains

Twelve units, each including:

- Listening and reading

  The dialogues and texts present real-life situations and language to help students understand the language of the catering industry.

- Vocabulary

  The vocabulary sections introduce and practise many useful words and expressions for professionals in the catering industry. All these terms are listed in a glossary at the back of the book.

- Language

  This section deals with both functional and grammatical structures. The functional language provides students with essential phrases for dealing with customers. The grammatical structures are always related to the communicative needs of professionals.

- Speechwork

  The pronunciation practice aims at increasing self-confidence when dealing with customers. Intonation, rhythm and stress are highlighted as essential for conveying the appropriate professional attitude – formality, politeness, respect and enthusiasm.

- Speaking

  Here students are asked to combine all they have learned – rather like serving a dish carefully prepared in advance.

Tips boxes

These include learning tips to help students learn more effectively, culture tips to make students think about how culture affects interactions with guests, and language tips to draw attention to particular language points.

Review units

Students and teachers can assess progress every four units through the grammar and vocabulary exercises in the review units. There are also communicative activities to evaluate oral perfomance.

Grammar reference section

This provides the basic grammar students need to ensure accurate language use.

Glossary

The glossary contains all the key vocabulary that appears in the coursebook plus other essential words. It is designed to become a personalised dictionary as students add translations in their own language.

Enjoy the cooking!

Anne Baude

Montserrat Iglesias

Anna Iñesta

Ready to Order **Bookmap**

The Casablanca Staff

Mr Grant the Manager

Susan the Head Waiter

Sam the Head Chef

Rosa a fish cook

Jan a waiter

Peter a bartender

Louis a pastry cook

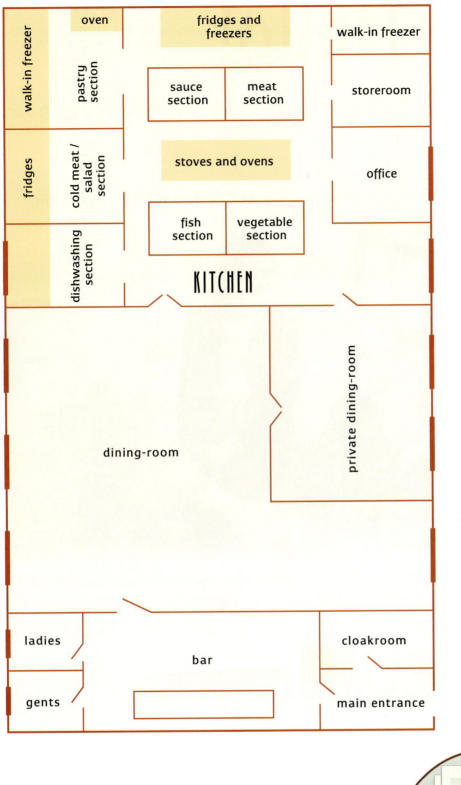

	oven	fridges and freezers		walk-in freezer
walk-in freezer	pastry section	sauce section	meat section	storeroom
fridges	cold meat / salad section	stoves and ovens		office
	dishwashing section	fish section	vegetable section	

KITCHEN

dining-room

private dining-room

ladies

bar

cloakroom

gents

main entrance

1 Hello!

Meet the boss

Speaking 1 Look at the picture below. Who are these people? Where are they?

🎧 **Listening** 2 Susan Davies, the Head Waiter at the Casablanca Restaurant, welcomes a new waiter. Listen and answer the questions opposite.

Susan	Good morning. My name's Susan Davies. I'm the Head Waiter. Welcome to the Casablanca.
Jan	Pleased to meet you. My name's Jan Nowak.
Susan	Before going to the restaurant I'd like to introduce you to Mr Grant, the Manager of the Hollywood Hotel.
Jan	The Hollywood Hotel?
Susan	Yes. The Casablanca Restaurant's part of the Hollywood Hotel. Here we are. Here's the Manager's office. Hi Jane. Is Mr Grant in his office?
Jane	Yes, he is.
Susan	Jan, this is Jane Newman, one of the hotel receptionists.
Jan	Nice to meet you. I'm Jan Nowak.
Jane	Hello, Jan. Nice to meet you.
Susan	Jan's the new waiter. Good morning, Mr Grant. Let me introduce you to Jan Nowak, the new waiter.

1 Who is Susan?
   a the new waiter   b the Head Waiter   c the Hotel Manager

2 Who is the hotel receptionist?
   a Jan   b Mr Grant   c Jane

3 Where is Mr Grant?
   a in the restaurant   b in his office   c at reception

Vocabulary

Greetings and introductions

3 Look at the dialogue and complete the table below.

Greeting	Introducing yourself	Introducing somebody
1 _Good morning_	3	5 ....
2	4	6 ....

4 What does Jan say in the following situations?

1 When Susan Davies introduces herself?
Pleased ....

2 When Susan Davies introduces Jane Newman? .... you.

Speaking

Asking for and giving personal information

5 What can you ask people when you meet them for the first time in your country? What can't you ask?

In my country you can ask about ...   But you can't ask about ...

6 Complete the CV with the words in the box.

Surname	Telephone number	Age	Nationality
Present job	Address	First name	

Titles

What are these titles in your language?

Mr _____
Mrs _____
Miss _____
Ms _____

Personal details

1   _Surname_   :   Nowak

2 .... :   Jan

3 .... :   37 St Dunstan's Road
                           South Norwood
                           London SE25 6EU

4 .... :   020 8248 6488

5 .... :   19

6 .... :   Polish

7 .... :   waiter

7 What information do these questions ask for?

Questions	Information
1 Where do you live?	.address........................
2 What's your first name?	....
3 What's your telephone number?	....
4 What do you do?	....
5 What's your surname?	....
6 How old are you?	....
7 Where are you from?	....

Vocabulary   Numbers

8 Match the words in the box to the pictures. Then practise saying the words.

| sign 1 | restaurant booking form | room key | restaurant bill | credit card |

What numbers are in the pictures?

Speechwork

9 Listen and practise saying these numbers.

0 zero	7 seven	14 fourteen	21 twenty-one
1 one	8 eight	15 fifteen	22 twenty-two
2 two	9 nine	16 sixteen	30 thirty
3 three	10 ten	17 seventeen	40 forty
4 four	11 eleven	18 eighteen	50 fifty
5 five	12 twelve	19 nineteen	100 a hundred
6 six	13 thirteen	20 twenty	

10 Listen to the telephone numbers. Tick the correct numbers and correct any mistakes you hear.

1) 0034 93 766544   ✔........   4) 0048 22 773155   ....

2) 0044 208 846771 ....   5) 0033 1 33 540338 ....

3) 001 262 566381   ....   6) 0030 1 337 3170 ....

Listening

11 Choose six of the room keys below. Listen to the numbers on the cassette. When you have heard all your six numbers shout 'Bingo'!

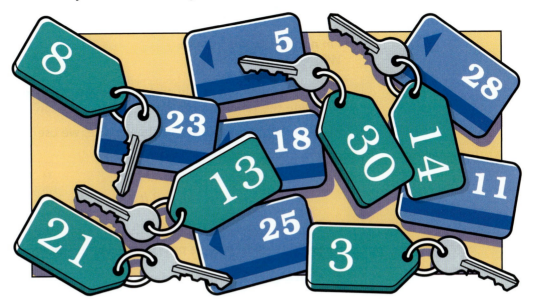

Speaking

12 Work in pairs. Ask questions and write a short CV about your partner.

Introducing colleagues

Listening

1 Sam Reilly, Head Chef of the Casablanca, introduces a new cook to his colleagues in the kitchen. Listen and complete the table below.

Times of day

Good evening is the usual greeting after six o'clock. *Good night* is used when people go to bed.

Rosa	Good evening everybody. Hi, Sam!
Sam	Hi, Rosa! Hey guys, this is Rosa, the new cook. She starts work tomorrow.
Peter	Hello Rosa. I'm Peter. Rosa's a charming name for a beautiful Italian lady…
Rosa	I'm not Italian, I'm Spanish!
Sam	Peter's the bartender. And this is Jan, the new waiter.
Rosa	Where are you from Jan?
Jan	I'm from Warsaw, in Poland.
Rosa	So many foreigners!
Peter	I'm British!
Jan	Are you British Sam?
Sam	No, I'm not. I'm from the US. And I make the best hamburger in London!
Peter	All right, Sam, we know that but fish and chips ~~is~~ are still the best!

Name	Job	Nationality
....	Head Chef	....
Rosa Gracia	....	....
Peter Cole	....	....
....	....	Polish

Language

The verb *be*

Look at these sentences and answer the questions.

*This **is** Rosa.*
*I'**m** **not** Italian, I'**m** Spanish.*
*Where **are** you from, Jan?*

Look at the dialogue again and underline the forms of the verb *be*. Then complete the following information.

*   With the present simple of the verb *be*, we use

    <u>am / ('m)</u> with *I*

    .... with *we*, *you* and *they*

    .... with *he*, *she* and *it*

*   To make negative sentences we put .... after the verb.
*   To make questions we put the .... before the person.

▶ **Check your answers on page 92.**

Practice

2 **Complete the text with the correct form of the verb *be*.**

Grammar tip

Only use *he* or *she* with people and animals. All non-living things are *it*.

Rosa and Sam ....<u>are</u>....¹ friends. They ....² British: Sam ....³ from the USA and Rosa ....⁴ Spanish. ....⁵ Sam from New York? No, he ....⁶ from New York, he ....⁷ from San Francisco. Rosa ....⁸ a cook at the Casablanca and her speciality ....⁹ fish. Her favourite dish ....¹⁰ paella. It ....¹¹ a traditional Spanish dish and it ....¹² very popular at the Casablanca.

3 **Complete the text with the correct form of the verb *be*.**

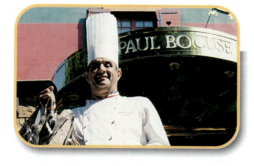

This .....<u>is</u>.....¹ Paul Bocuse.

He ....² a famous French chef.

He ....³ the father of *nouvelle cuisine*.

They ....⁴ two famous bartenders.

They ....⁵ very popular with women.

................⁶ they good at making cocktails?

Vocabulary — Countries and nationalities

4 Match the food and drink to the correct country.

Paella is a Spanish dish.
Caviare is a Russian speciality.

1 paella
2 hamburger
3 port
4 guinness
5 chocolates
6 caviare
7 wine and cheese
8 sushi
9 giros
10 pasta

Speechwork

5 Put the countries and nationalities in the correct word stress groups.

Dutch	Portugal	France	Chinese	Portuguese
British	Ireland	American	Italian	Spain
Japan	Italy	Russian	Belgium	Greece

1 ☐
Dutch
....

....

....

....

2 ☐☐
British
....

....

....

....

3 ☐☐
Japan
....

....

4 ☐☐☐
Portugal
....

....

5 ☐☐☐
....

6 ☐☐☐
....

7 ☐☐☐☐
....

Listen and check your answers. Then practise saying the words.

Speaking

6 Your teacher will give you a card and a questionnaire. Imagine you are the person on your card. Introduce yourself and find the other people on the questionnaire.

2 A new job

First day at work

Speaking

1 **What do these words mean? What are they in your language?**

speak	arrive	show	prepare	attend	serve	drink

Listening

2 **Rosa arrives for her first day at work. Listen and answer the questions below.**

Rosa   Good morning!

Peter   *Buenos dias*, Rosa.

Rosa   Do you speak Spanish?

Peter   Not really. But I can speak French.

Rosa   Oh right. Is Sam here?

Peter   No, he always arrives late. Can I show you the restaurant?

Rosa   Oh, yes, please.

Peter   Well, this is the reception area, with the cloakroom next to it, and here's the bar, where I work.

Rosa   Do you work alone in the bar?

Peter   Yes. I prepare all the drinks, attend the customers at the bar and serve drinks to the tables. Would you like a coffee?

Rosa   No, thanks, I don't drink coffee. Can you show me the dining-room?

Peter   Sure. No, not that way: they're the toilets. The dining-room's on the right.

Rosa   Oh, it's really nice!

Peter   And there's a small private dining-room over there.

1 Does Peter speak Spanish?
2 Is Sam in the kitchen?
3 Does Peter have a lot of work?

4 Does Rosa have a coffee?
5 Is there only one dining-room?

Speechwork

3 Listen to these sentences and underline the stressed word.

1 a) Do you speak <u>Spanish</u>?
  b) Do <u>you</u> speak Spanish?

2 a) Is Sam here?
  b) Is Sam here?

3 a) He always arrives late.
  b) He always arrives late.

4 a) I don't drink coffee.
  b) I don't drink coffee.

5 a) These are the toilets.
  b) These are the toilets.

6 a) The dining-room's on the right.
  b) The dining-room's on the right.

Now work in pairs. Student A choose a pair of sentences and say one of the sentences. Student B say which sentence you hear.

Parts of the restaurant

Vocabulary

4 Complete the diagram with the words in the box. Use a dictionary to help you.

| smoking section | kitchen | fish section | dining-room |
| cloakroom | sauce section | toilets | meat section |

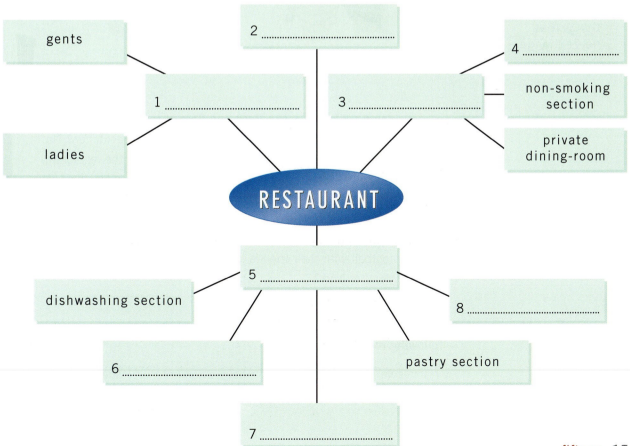

gents

2 ....

4 ....

1 ....

3 ....

non-smoking section

private dining-room

ladies

RESTAURANT

5 ....

dishwashing section

8 ....

6 ....

pastry section

7 ....

Language

Present simple

Look at these sentences and answer the questions.

positive	*negative*	*question*
a) I **get** really tired.	c) I **don't drink** coffee.	e) **Do** you **speak** Spanish?
b) He **gets** really tired.	d) He **doesn't drink** coffee.	f) **Does** he **speak** Spanish?

- What is the difference between the form of the verb in sentences (a) and (b)?
- Which verb is the same form in sentences (c) and (d)?
- What is the difference between positive and negative sentences?
- What is the first word in sentences (e) and (f)?
- What do you find in negative sentences and questions but not in positive sentences?

▶ **Check your answers on page 92.**

Practice

5 **Complete the text with the correct form of the present simple.**

Language tip

The present simple describes things that happen again and again or things that never change.

Jan *work / works* ¹ with Rosa and Sam at the Casablanca
Restaurant. *Do / Does* ² he work with them in the kitchen? No,
he *don't / doesn't* ³ work in the same section of the restaurant.
He *serve / serves* ⁴ the guests in the dining-room. Jan *like / likes* ⁵
his job very much because he *deal / deals* ⁶ with different people
every day. When Sam and Jan *finish / finishes* ⁷ work in the
afternoon, they *don't / doesn't* ⁸ go home. They *play / plays* ⁹
football with their friends in the park. What *do / does* ¹⁰ you
do after work?

Speaking

6 **Work in pairs. Student A turn to page 90. Student B make questions with the following information.**

like cola	work in a bar	have a computer	speak a foreign language
	live in a small village	watch TV a lot	sleep a lot

Now ask each other the questions you have prepared. Take notes of your partner's answers and then report them to the rest of the class.

B: Do you like cola?
A: Yes, I do / No, I don't.   B: He likes / doesn't like cola.

The workplace

Vocabulary

1 **Put the words in the box in the correct groups. Use a dictionary to help you.**

head chef	fish section	freezer	rolls	cocktails	cook
grill	pastry cook	pastry section	croissants		deep-fryer
desserts	vegetable section	oven	stove	fridge	commis

Jobs	Sections in the kitchen	Appliances	Food and drinks
head chef	fish section	freezer	rolls

Listening

2 **Sam shows Rosa the kitchen. Listen and say whether the sentences below are true or false.**

Sam So, what do you think of the restaurant, Rosa?

Rosa Well, it's very nice, but I'd like to see the kitchen.

Sam Come with me, then. Louis, Karl, let me introduce you to Rosa. Rosa's the new cook. She's in charge of the fish section.

Louis I'm Louis the pastry cook and Karl works with me in the pastry section.

Sam Karl's the commis. In the mornings he helps me to bake rolls and croissants for breakfast and then he prepares desserts. But he can help you at lunch-time.

Rosa Oh, great! And where's the fish section?

Sam It's over here, next to the vegetable section.

Rosa Is there an oven and stove just for the fish cook?

Sam There's an oven here just for you but there isn't a stove. There are four stoves in the middle and you share them with the other cooks.

Rosa OK, that's fine. It all looks great.

1 Rosa likes the restaurant.
2 Rosa is a fish cook.
3 Louis and Karl prepare rolls and croissants for dessert.
4 Louis can assist Rosa.
5 Rosa shares an oven with the other cooks.

Now correct any false sentences.

Vocabulary

Jobs

3 Complete the diagram with the words in the box. Then practise saying the words.

head waiter	dining-room assistant	head chef	salad cook
meat cook	sauce cook	pastry cook	waiter

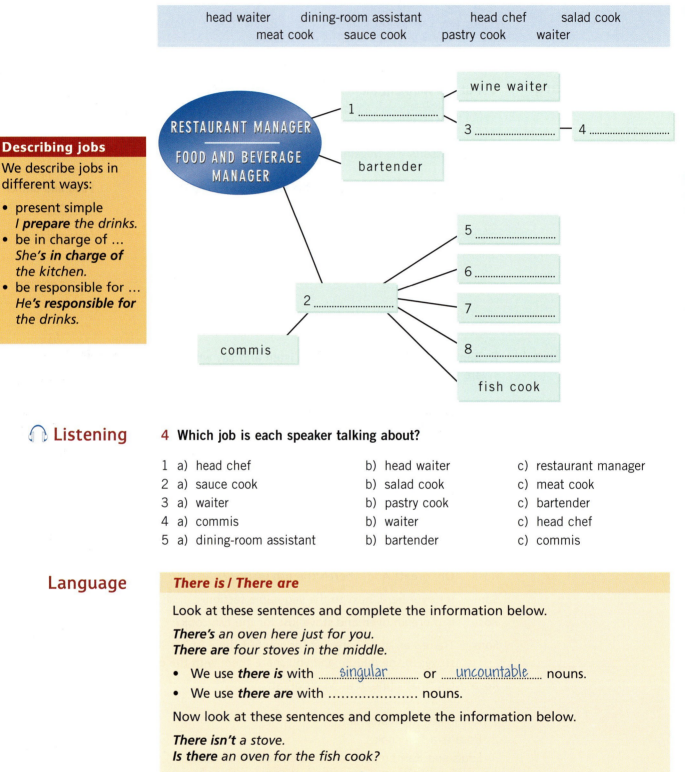

RESTAURANT MANAGER — FOOD AND BEVERAGE MANAGER

wine waiter

1 ....

3 .... — 4 ....

bartender

5 ....

6 ....

2 ....

7 ....

8 ....

commis

fish cook

Describing jobs

We describe jobs in different ways:

• present simple
*I **prepare** the drinks.*
• be in charge of …
*She's **in charge of** the kitchen.*
• be responsible for …
*He's **responsible for** the drinks.*

🎧 Listening

4 Which job is each speaker talking about?

1 a) head chef b) head waiter c) restaurant manager
2 a) sauce cook b) salad cook c) meat cook
3 a) waiter b) pastry cook c) bartender
4 a) commis b) waiter c) head chef
5 a) dining-room assistant b) bartender c) commis

Language

There is / There are

Look at these sentences and complete the information below.

***There's** an oven here just for you.*
***There are** four stoves in the middle.*

• We use ***there is*** with ....singular.......... or ....uncountable...... nouns.
• We use ***there are*** with .... nouns.

Now look at these sentences and complete the information below.

***There isn't** a stove.*
***Is there** an oven for the fish cook?*

• We make questions with ....is........ ***there*** or ***are*** ....
• We make negative sentences with ***there*** .... or ***there*** ....aren't... .

▶ **Check your answers on page 93.**

Practice

5 Complete the description of the kitchen with *there is / there are*.

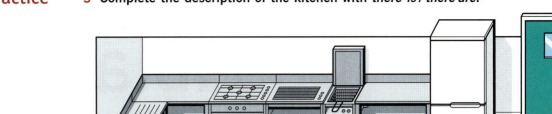

There are ¹ many things in this kitchen. On the left, ... ² a stove next to the grill. On the right of the grill .... ³ a deep-fryer. The grill is between the stove and the deep-fryer. The fridge and freezer are near the door. The freezer is under the fridge. .... ⁴ croissants in the oven. .... ⁵ a table in the middle of the kitchen. .... ⁶ three things on the table.

6 Match the words in the box to the pictures. Then practise saying the words.

| next to   in   on   under   on the left of   on the right of   in the middle of |

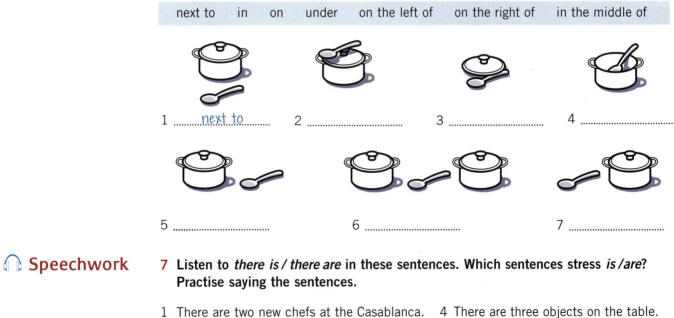

1 .... _next to_ ....   2 ....   3 ....   4 ....

5 ....   6 ....   7 ....

⌢⌣ Speechwork

7 Listen to *there is / there are* in these sentences. Which sentences stress *is / are*? Practise saying the sentences.

1 There are two new chefs at the Casablanca.
2 There's an oven in the pastry section.
3 There isn't a fridge in the meat section.
4 There are three objects on the table.
5 There aren't any guests in the bar.

Speaking

8 Work in pairs. Student A turn to page 86. Student B turn to page 88. Find five differences between your picture and your partner's.

In my picture there is / are ...   Is there a ... in your picture?
There isn't a / any ... in my picture.   Where is the ... in your picture?

3 The Casablanca

An enquiry

1 **What do guests ask about when they phone a restaurant?**

2 **Jan answers the Casablanca phone. Listen and answer the questions below.**

Jan Good morning, Casablanca Restaurant. Can I help you?

Ms Porter Yes, you can. My name's Georgina Porter. I'm getting married. It's my fifth wedding, and I'd like a banquet. I'm not planning a large banquet, just a small party for twenty-five people.

Jan We have a private dining-room for thirty people – the Bergman Lounge.

Ms Porter Oh that's great! And where exactly is the …

Jan The Casablanca madam. The address is 5 Hanover Street.

Ms Porter Oh, and where's that? I'm from the States, you see. I live in Maryland.

Jan But where are you staying in London madam?

Ms Porter Oh, yes. I'm staying at the Queen Victoria Hotel, near Oxford Circus. So, how can I get to your restaurant?

Jan It's very easy madam. Go along Regent Street in the direction of Piccadilly Circus. Pass Princes Street, then turn right into Hanover Street and go straight on for about 100 metres. The restaurant is on your right.

Ms Porter OK. That's great. Thank you very much.

1 What does Ms Porter want?
2 How many people can eat in the Bergman Lounge?
3 Where is Ms Porter from?
4 Where is Ms Porter staying at the moment?
5 What street is the Casablanca in?

Vocabulary *Wh-* words

3 Match the questions with the answers.

1 What do you do?
2 Who is that man?
3 Where is the toilet?
4 When do you open?
5 How are you?
6 Why are you nervous?

a) Fine, thanks.
b) I'm a waiter.
c) It's my wedding day.
d) It's near the entrance.
e) At eleven o'clock.
f) He is the bartender.

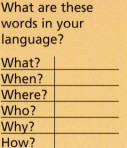

Grammar tip
What are these words in your language?

What?	
When?	
Where?	
Who?	
Why?	
How?	

Speechwork

4 Now listen to the questions and underline the stressed words. Which words are stressed in *wh-* questions? Practise asking the questions.

Listening Seating arrangements

5 Susan and Jan discuss the seating for a banquet. Put all the words in the correct groups, then listen and tick the words you hear.

small	oval	large	conference style	medium-sized	square
banqueting style	round	horseshoe / U-shape	rectangular		

table size	table shape	seating arrangement
small		

Now use the words to describe the following seating arrangements.

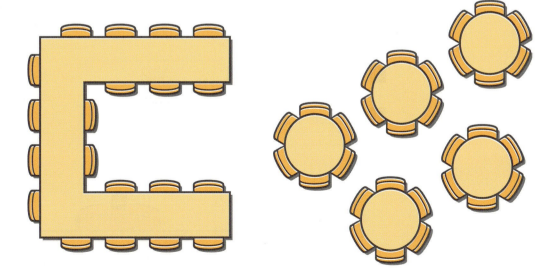

Speaking

6 Work in pairs. Student A turn to page 86. Student B turn to page 88. Draw a picture of the seating arrangement your partner describes to you.

Language

Present continuous

Look at these sentences and answer the questions.

I'm staying at the Queen Victoria Hotel.
I live in Maryland.

• Which sentence talks about a permanent state? (present simple)
• Which sentence talks about what is happening now? (present continuous)

Now look at these sentences and complete the information below.

I'm not planning a large banquet.
Where *are you staying* in London, madam?

• We make negative sentences by putting *not/n't* between the verb ....be.......... and the .... form of the main verb.

• We make questions by putting the **subject** between the verb .... and the .... form of the main verb.

▶ **Check your answers on page 93.**

Speaking

7 Work in groups of four. Student A turn to page 86, student B to page 87, student C to page 89 and student D to page 90. Ask questions to find out where the following guests are sitting and what they are eating.

Where is Mr Jones sitting?   *What is Mr Spencer eating?*

Mr Jones	Mr Collins	Mr Spencer	Mrs Robinson
Mrs Jones	Mr Thorpe	Mrs Clark	Mrs Edwards

1 Mr Jones
  hamburger

2 ....

3 ....

4 ....

5 ....
....

6 Mr Spencer
....

7 ....

8 ....

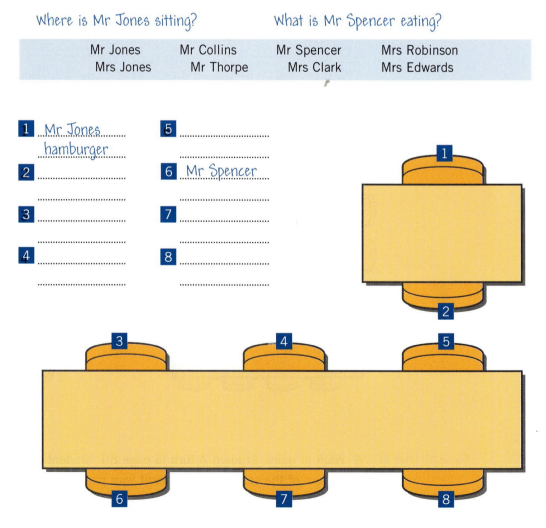

Giving directions

🎧 **Listening**

1 Rosa has a day off tomorrow and wants to go shopping. She asks her colleagues for advice. Listen and complete the table below.

	Rosa	Peter	Jan
1 Who doesn't have plans for tomorrow?		✓	
2 Who wants to go to Carnaby Street tomorrow?			
3 Who gives directions to Carnaby Street?			
4 Who is going to Carnaby Street tomorrow?			

2 Look at the dialogue and the map. Who gives the correct directions?

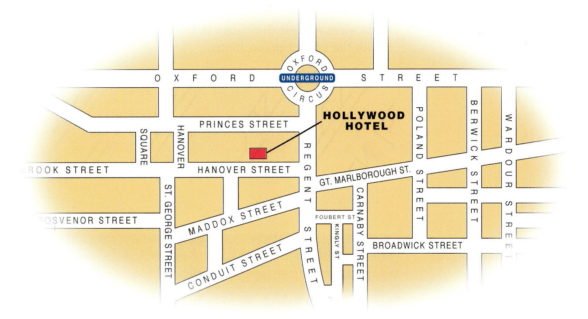

Peter So, Rosa. What are your plans for tomorrow? I'm free all day!

Rosa Well, I'd like to go shopping tomorrow. I need a gift for a friend.

Peter Is it a boy or a girl?

Rosa A boy.

Peter Is he a special friend?

Rosa All my friends are special. Anyway, where can I find a nice gift?

Sam You could go to Carnaby Street. There are lots of gift shops there.

Rosa How do I get to Carnaby Street?

Jan You go out of the restaurant and turn left. Go straight on and turn right into Regent Street. Walk along Regent Street and turn left into Foubert Street. Pass Kingly and take the first street on the right. That's Carnaby Street.

Peter That's not right. You turn right into Regent Street, and then left into Foubert Street. Turn into Kingly and then Carnaby Street is at the end of Kingly Street. I know! I'm from London! I can come with you Rosa to show you the way.

Jan Yes, we can all come!

Rosa Thanks guys, but I can find it on my own. There are street maps at reception.

Vocabulary — Verbs of movement

3 Match the words in the box to the pictures. Then practise saying the words.

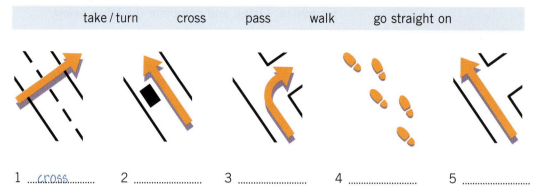

| take / turn | cross | pass | walk | go straight on |

1 ...cross.........   2 ....   3 ....   4 ....   5 ....

4 Jan gives a guest directions to the chemist. Complete Jan's directions with the correct prepositions.

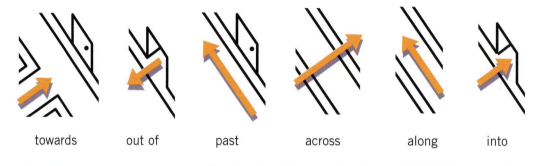

towards   out of   past   across   along   into

> To get to the chemist, you go (1) *out of / into* the restaurant and walk (2) *along / past* Hanover Street (3) *towards / out of* Regent Street. Go (4) *across / past* the supermarket and then walk (5) *into / out of* the next building. It's a large shopping centre. The chemist is (6) *towards / across* the hall.

5 Look at Jan's directions from Oxford Circus to the Casablanca. Mark the Casablanca on the map.

> It's very easy, madam. Take Regent Street in the direction of Piccadilly Circus. Pass Princes Street, then turn right into Hanover Street and go straight on for about 100 metres. The restaurant is on your right.

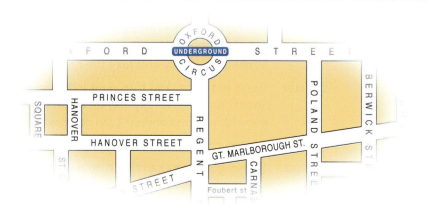

🎧 Speechwork   Asking the way

6 Listen to these sentences. Mark where the speaker's voice is high and low. Then practise saying the sentences.

Excuse me, I'm looking for Carnaby Street. Can you help me?

Yes, I can. You go straight on and then ...

I'm sorry, I can't help you.

Speaking

7 Work in pairs. Student A turn to page 89. Student B look at the map of Fisherman's Wharf in San Francisco and follow the instructions. You work at the Tourist Information Center on the corner of Jefferson Street and Mason Street. Give your partner directions to the places he/she asks for.

Now swap roles and ask for directions to these places:

- The Silver Anchor Restaurant in The Anchorage shopping center.
- The Alcatraz ferry ticket office.
- The Wax Museum on Jefferson Street.
- The Fish Alley.

Directions by train

These phrases are useful for giving directions on the underground (UK) or subway (US):

Go to ... station
Take the ... line to ...
Change at ...
Get off at ...

Boudin Sourdough Bakery
produces the tangy bread for which San francisco is famous.

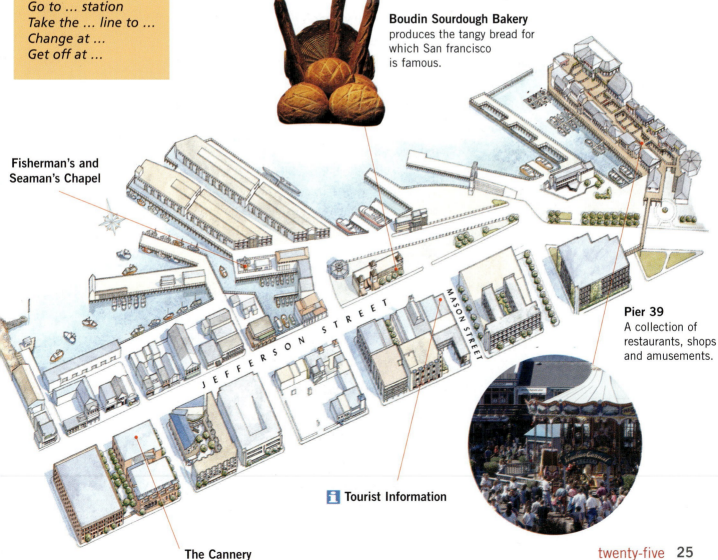

Fisherman's and Seaman's Chapel

JEFFERSON STREET

MASON STREET

Pier 39
A collection of restaurants, shops and amusements.

ℹ️ Tourist Information

The Cannery

4 Reservations

Taking reservations

Speaking 1 What information do you ask for when taking a reservation?

🎧 Listening 2 Jan answers the telephone at the Casablanca. Listen and check the booking form below. Correct any mistakes.

Jan	Good afternoon, Casablanca Restaurant. Can I help you?
Mr Russell	I'd like to reserve a table, please.
Jan	Certainly sir. For what day, please?
Mr Russell	For today.
Jan	OK, so that's the 7th. And what time?
Mr Russell	Half seven, please.
Jan	And for how many people?
Mr Russell	Just two, please.
Jan	Is that smoking or non-smoking?
Mr Russell	Non-smoking.
Jan	OK sir, that's no problem. And what name is it, please?
Mr Russell	Russell.
Jan	Could you spell that, please sir?
Mr Russell	Yes, it's R-U-double S-E-double L.
Jan	Thank you. So, that's a table for two at seven-thirty this evening. Thank you very much Mr Russell. See you this evening.
Mr Russell	That's great. Thanks. Bye.

Casablanca

Name: Mrs Brussell

Date: 6 July

Time: 6.30

Number of people 7

(Non) / Smoking

Language

Reservations

Note we can say:

*book a table
reserve a table
make a booking
make a
  reservation*

Making bookings

3 **Look at the dialogue again. What does Jan say to get the following information?**

1) name   *What name is it please?* ...... 4) number of people ....

2) day   .... 5) smoking ....

3) time   .... 6) spelling ....

Now find the phrases Jan uses to:

7) answer the phone   ....

8) say 'OK' in a formal way   ....

9) check the information   ....

Listening

4 **Listen to two dialogues and complete the booking forms.**

Casablanca

Name: __mrs Kerrigan__

Date: (1) _____

Time: (2) _____

No. of people (3) _____

Casablanca

Name: __mr fox__

Date: (4) _____

Time: (5) _____

No. of people (6) _____

Speechwork

The alphabet

5 **Look at the words below. Each letter of the alphabet sounds the same as the vowel sound of one of these words. Put the letters of the alphabet in the correct groups and then listen to check your answers.**

they	me	ten	my	no	you	are
a	b	f	i	o	g	r
	c					

6 **Work in pairs. Choose words from the glossary on pages 104–111 and spell them to your partner. Write down the words your partner spells and then check your answers.**

🎧 **Listening**   Clock times

7 Look at the information below. Then listen and tick (✓) the correct times.

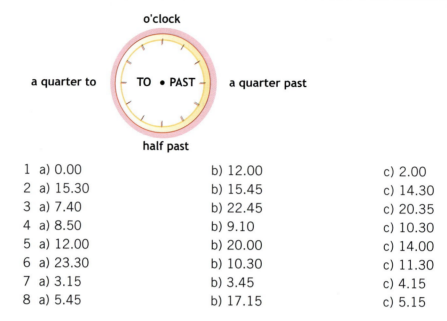

1	a) 0.00	b) 12.00	c) 2.00
2	a) 15.30	b) 15.45	c) 14.30
3	a) 7.40	b) 22.45	c) 20.35
4	a) 8.50	b) 9.10	c) 10.30
5	a) 12.00	b) 20.00	c) 14.00
6	a) 23.30	b) 10.30	c) 11.30
7	a) 3.15	b) 3.45	c) 4.15
8	a) 5.45	b) 17.15	c) 5.15

Speaking

8 Work in pairs. Student A turn to page 90, student B look at the clocks below. Tell your partner the time and write down the times your partner tells you.

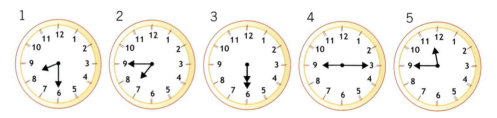

9 Work in pairs. Use the information to write a dialogue. Practise your dialogue and then read it to the class.

Waiter at Carlo's Pizzeria

Answer the phone

Ask when for

Ask what time

Ask how many people

Ask for the name

Check details / spelling
Thank guest for calling

Guest

Ask to book a table

Give a day / date

Give a time

Say how many people

Give a name and spell it

Thank waiter, say goodbye

The Casablanca Restaurant

Speaking   1   **Where can you find out information about the best places to eat?**

Reading   2   **Read the advertisement for the Casablanca and answer the guest's questions.**

5 Hanover Street London WIA 4BZ
Tel. 020 7734 7002 Fax. 020 7734 6437

Set in the heart of London, five minutes from Oxford Circus. Enjoy a wonderful meal in the relaxed atmosphere of our renowned restaurant.

International cuisine

A varied choice of fresh food on our à la carte menu

Table d'hôte menu

available at lunch-time

Children's menu

Traditional English breakfast

from 7 to 10 in the morning

Special prices for Christmas banquets in December

Excellent service

Free car parking

Closed on Tuesdays in winter

Bookings advisable

www.hotelhollywood.co.uk

1   Is your restaurant in Oxford Street?
2   Are there only British specialities on your menu?
3   Can we have a table d'hôte meal for dinner?
4   My son is eight years old. Do you have special dishes for him?
5   Do you only serve breakfast to English people?
6   I'd like to have a special meal for Christmas. Is it possible at the Casablanca?
7   Do I have to pay to park my car?
8   Is the restaurant open every day all year round?

Vocabulary

Days, months and seasons

3 Complete the table with words from the Casablanca advertisement.

Menus	1	_à la carte_	Days of the week	6	
	2		Parts of the day	7	
	3		Months	8	
Daily meals	4		Seasons	9	
	5				

4 🎧 Tick the days and months that you hear.

Monday	....	January	....	August	....
Tuesday	✓	February	....	September	....
Wednesday	....	March	....	October	....
Thursday	....	April	....	November	....
Friday	....	May	....	December	....
Saturday	....	June	....		
Sunday	....	July	....		

5 Look at the traditional UK and continental breakfasts below. Match the names to the pictures. Use a dictionary to help you.

milk **10** croissant   coffee   jam   eggs   pastries   mushrooms   fruit juice
bacon   cold meat   grapefruit   toast   cereals   tea   sausages   tomato   rolls

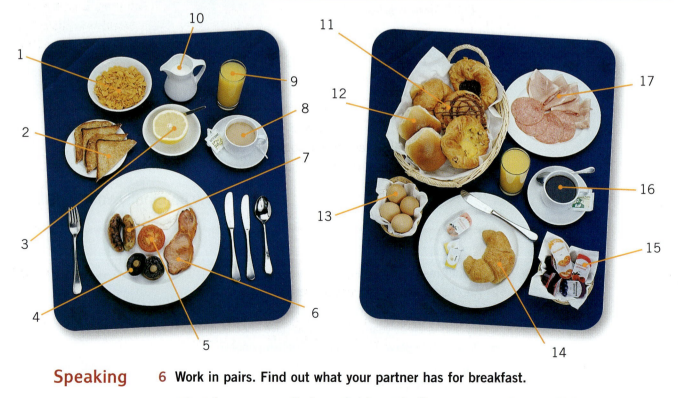

Speaking

6 Work in pairs. Find out what your partner has for breakfast.

A: What do you normally have for breakfast?   **B:** I normally have ...

Language

Prepositions of time

Look at the prepositions in these sentences.

a) *Traditional English breakfast available **from** 7 **to** 10 a.m.*
b) *Special prices for Christmas banquets **in** December.*
c) *Closed **in** winter.*
d) *A table for two **at** seven o'clock this evening.*
e) *I'm sorry madam, but the restaurant closes **in** the evening.*
f) *All right, so that's a table for two **on** Saturday.*

Now match the sentences with these rules.

1 We use *in* with seasons. ....c...
2 We use *at* with times. ....
3 We use *on* with days. ....
4 We use *in* with parts of the day. ....
5 We use *in* with months. ....
6 We use *from* and *to* to show the beginning and end of something. ....

▶ **Check your answers on page 94.**

Practice

7 Complete the text with the correct prepositions. You can use the same preposition more than once.

in	at	on	from	to

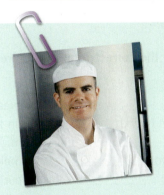

This is Sam, our Head Chef. He's very busy, because he prepares all the meals at the Casablanca. He arrives at the restaurant ....at..........[1] 9.00 ....[2] the morning. He's especially busy ....[3] lunch-time. Lunch is served ....[4] 12.00 ....[5] 14.00 every day. The restaurant is open ....[6] Tuesday ....[7] Sunday. On Saturday evening the restaurant is usually full, so Sam starts preparing the dishes ....[8] the afternoon. ....[9] Sunday he prepares a special meal. Sam always prepares a delicious cake for his birthday. His birthday is ....[10] November. ....[11] autumn he usually prepares his speciality: *marrons glacés*. ....[12] September Sam goes away on holiday. He always says he needs it!

Casablanca

Speaking

8 Work in pairs. Find out when your partner does the things below and then read your answers to the rest of the class.

wake up	have breakfast	get dressed	go to work	have lunch
go out	have dinner	watch TV	go to bed	

A: When do you wake up?   B: I wake up at seven-thirty. How about you?

Review

1 Put these sentences in the correct order to complete the dialogue.

a) ☐ **Waiter** Could you spell that, please?

b) ☐ **Guest** Good afternoon. I'd like to book a table.

c) ☐ **Waiter** So that's a table for three at eight o'clock next Friday. Thank you, Mr Graham.

d) ☐ **Guest** For next Friday.

e) ☐ **Guest** At eight o'clock, please.

f) ☐ **Waiter** Eight o'clock's fine. What name is it, please?

g) ☐ **Guest** For three people.

h) ☐ **Waiter** Certainly, sir. For what day, please?

i) ☐ **Waiter** What time would you like to come?

j) ☐ **Guest** Graham.

k) ☐ **Waiter** For how many people would that be?

l) ☐ **Guest** Yes, it's G-R-A-H-A-M.

m) **1** **Waiter** Good afternoon, St Remy Restaurant. Can I help you?

n) ☐ **Guest** Thank you. Goodbye.

2 Complete the sentences with the correct form of the present simple or present continuous.

1 At the moment we (*lay*) ...... *are laying* ...... the tables for breakfast.

2 During the week Paul and Joan (*work*) .... in the kitchen, but this afternoon they (*help*) .... in the dining-room.

3 What (*cook*) .... you ....? It smells delicious!

4 The bartender always (*prepare*) .... his favourite cocktail for Mrs Hamilton, but now he (*make*) .... a new cocktail for her.

5 The Head Waiter usually (*welcome*) .... the guests, but today he (*not do*) .... it because he's ill.

6 What (*do*) .... the reception waiter ....? There's nobody at the reception desk!

7 (*like*) .... Patrick .... spaghetti? No, he (*not like*) .... Italian food.

8 (*live*) .... you .... in Paris? No, I (*not like*) .... large cities. But my brother (*live*) .... in Paris.

3 Complete the text with the words in the box.

on	in	from	to	next to	at	in	in	next to	on

There's a new restaurant ...... *next to* ......[1] my house. It is open ....[2] 9.00 ....[3] 16.00 ....[4] winter. ....[5] the evening it opens again ....[6] 19.00, but only ....[7] July and August. There is a car park ....[8] the restaurant, ...[9] the right. The car park is closed ....[10] Mondays.

4 Which word is different? Underline it.

1) U-shaped	fridge	stove	grill
2) morning	supper	evening	afternoon
3) freezer	horseshoe	deep-fryer	oven
4) lunch	dinner	breakfast	banqueting style
5) dining-room	bar	kitchen	small
6) Italian	France	Dutch	Greek
7) commis	chef	butter	waiter
8) spring	roll	toast	jam

5 Look at the map of Rye. Read these directions and match the places to the numbers on the map.

Town Hall	The Mermaid Inn	Post Office	Old Grammar School	The Market

1 Go out of the railway station and turn left. Go along the street and the market is on the right.

2 Go out of the railway station and walk straight on. Then take the first street on the right and the post office is on your right.

3 Go out of the railway station and walk straight on. Go past Cinque Ports street and take the next left. Walk along and the Old Grammar School is on your left.

4 Go out of the railway station and turn right. Then turn left into Ferry Road. Turn right at the end of the road and walk straight on. Take the first left and walk straight on. Pass The Mint and the Mermaid Inn is on your left.

5 Go out of the railway station and walk straight on. Pass the first left and take the next one. Then take the first right and walk to the end of the street. The town hall is in front of you.

6 Work in pairs. Give each other directions to places in Rye.

5 Welcome!

Receiving guests

🎧 Listening

1 **What do you do when you receive guests?**

2 Jan receives two guests at the Casablanca. Look at the list of actions on the opposite page then listen and tick the things he does.

Jan	Good evening madam. Good evening sir. Do you have a reservation?
Mr Kerrigan	Yes, we do.
Jan	Could I have the name, please?
Mr Kerrigan	Mr and Mrs Kerrigan.
Jan	One moment, yes, Mr and Mrs Kerrigan – table for two. Shall I take your coats?
Mr Kerrigan	Yes, please. Can I leave my hat, too?
Jan	Certainly. Would you prefer to sit indoors or outdoors?
Mrs Kerrigan	I think we'd prefer indoors. What about the small table near the piano?
Jan	I'm very sorry madam. I'm afraid that table is not available. But the round one near the window is free.
Mr Kerrigan	Perfect. That's fine.
Jan	Follow me, please. I'll show you to your table.
Mr Kerrigan	Thank you.
Jan	Here's the menu.

1	Greet the guests	✓	_Good evening madam._
2	Ask if there is a booking	....	....
3	Ask for the name	....	....
4	Check the booking details	....	....
5	Offer the guests a coffee	....	....
6	Offer cloakroom service	....	....
7	Offer a choice of seats	....	....
8	Apologise and explain problem	....	....
9	Suggest seats	....	....
10	Show the kitchen to the guests	....	....
11	Show the guests to their table	....	....
12	Present the menu	....	....

Now listen again and write the phrases Jan uses. Then practise saying them.

Language

Modal verbs

Modal verbs such as *can, could, will, would, may* and *shall* are special because:

- they never change their form
  I'll show you to your table. (I'll = I will)
  He'll show you to your table. (He'll = He will)

- their negative and question forms do not use *do / does*
  I'm afraid you can't sit there, the table's reserved.
  Shall I take your coat?

- they are not followed by *to*
  ~~We can't to sit here.~~

  Underline the modal verbs in the conversation on the opposite page.

▶ **For more information see page 94.**

Practice

3 Choose the correct option to complete these useful restaurant phrases.

1 _Could_ / _Shall_ I have your name, please?

2 _Would_ / _Shall_ I take your coats?

3 _Would_ / _May_ you prefer to sit indoors or outdoors?

4 _May_ / _Will_ I suggest the terrace?

5 _Shall_ / _Can_ we order, please?

6 _Would_ / _Shall_ you like to take a seat?

7 _I'll_ / _may_ show you to your table.

8 _Would_ / _Will_ you like to see the wine list?

9 I'm afraid you _won't_ / _can't_ smoke here.

10 _Can_ / _May_ you follow me, please?

Learner tip

Remember to keep a record of all the useful phrases you learn.

Vocabulary

Parts of the dining-room

4 Match the words in the box to the picture. Then practise saying the words.

terrace **7**	smoking section	piano	window	indoors	
outdoors	bar	corner	dance floor	non-smoking section	

Listening

5 Now listen to the dialogue and tick the areas you hear.

Speechwork

6 Tick the words that you hear. Then make sentences with the ticked words.

1 a) should ✓
  b) could
2 a) take
  b) make
3 a) label
  b) table
4 a) talk
  b) walk

5 a) round
  b) pound
6 a) large
  b) March
7 a) could
  b) would
8 a) shake
  b) shape

9 a) cook
  b) book
10 a) more
  b) floor
11 a) stair
  b) square
12 a) turn
  b) burn

Speaking

7 Work in two teams. Team A choose a table from the seating plan above. Team B ask *Yes / No* questions to find out which table it is.

A Is it near the piano?
B Yes, it is.

A Is it a round table?
B No, it isn't.

A wedding banquet

Listening

1 Jan is preparing a wedding banquet at the Casablanca. Susan calls him to check the preparations. Listen and say whether the sentences are true or false.

1 The tables are in banqueting style.
2 Jan is going to use a pink tablecloth.
3 Jan is going to set out 100 plates.
4 Susan tells Jan to use the Venetian crystal.
5 The Venetian champagne glasses go with the Limoges plates.

Jan – I'm going to arrive late today. Please start getting the Bergman Lounge ready:

- *number of guests: 25*
- *table arrangements: U-shape*
- *tablecloth: linen (pink). Check with laundry.*
- *dinner plates, soup plates, side plates and dessert plates (Limoges)*
- *glasses: water, red and white wine*
- *crystal champagne glasses – check the Venetian glasses are OK*
- *fish and meat cutlery, and soup spoons*

Jan Hello, Casablanca Restaurant.

Susan Jan, it's Susan. How's it going? Is everything ready for the banquet?

Jan Well, the tables are ready, in a U-shape, and now I'm going to lay them.

Susan Great. What tablecloth are you going to use?

Jan I got the pink linen from the laundry, and the napkins.

Susan Good. And do we have enough plates?

Jan Yes, I'm going to use the Limoges plates: twenty-five dinner plates, twenty-five side plates and twenty-five dessert plates and twenty-five soup plates.

Susan Fine. What glasses are you going to use? The Venetian?

Jan No, I'm not going to use the Venetian ones – we've only got twenty of them.

Susan Which ones are you going to use then? The Bohemian?

Jan That's right. They go with the Limoges plates perfectly.

Susan Excellent Jan! You seem to have everything under control. Well done.

Language

▶ Check your answers on page 95.

Going to + verb

Look at these sentences and answer the questions.

***I'm going to use** the Limoges plates.*
***I'm not going to use** the Venetian glasses.*
*Which glasses **are you going to use**?*

- Do these sentences refer to the past, present or future?
- Which two words can you find in all three sentences?

Look for examples of negative sentences and questions in the dialogue. How do we form negative sentences and questions with ***going to*** + verb?

▶ **Check your answers on page 95.**

Going to + verb is used to talk about future plans and predictions.

***I'm going to visit** my family next week.*
***We're not going to have** enough champagne glasses for all the guests.*

Practice

2 **Look at the pictures and make sentences saying what these people are going to do.**

1) Olga / go shopping ....*Olga is going to go shopping*....
2) Paulo and Bianca / have a romantic dinner ....
3) Maria / see a movie ....
4) Thomas and Alfonso / play football ....

3 **Work in groups. Find out the other students' plans for the weekend. When you finish, report them to the rest of the class.**

Example: A *What are you going to do at the weekend, Antonio?*
B *I'm going to play football.*
B *Antonio is going to play football at the weekend.*

You	
Student A	
Student B	
Student C	
Student D	

Tableware for lunch and dinner

4 Match the words in the box to the pictures. Then practise saying the words.

> salt/pepper pot **4**   dinner plate   ashtray   fork   napkin   knife   slipcloth
> side plate   soup spoon   glass   tablecloth   dessert spoon   soup bowl

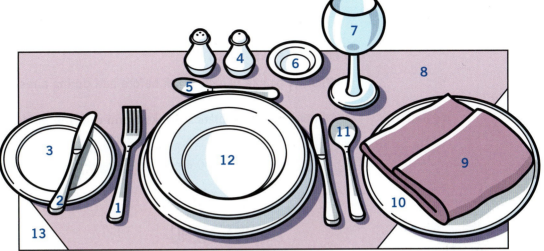

Tableware for breakfast

5 Match the words in the box to the tableware. Then practise saying the words.

> teapot **3**   saucer   sugar pot   coffee pot   tray
> milk jug   cup   cereal bowl   teaspoon   dessert spoon

Listening

6 You are going to prepare a breakfast tray. Listen and draw the tray.

Speaking

7 Work in pairs. Draw a breakfast tray with all of the above items on it and then describe it to your partner. Draw your partner's tray.

Example: A Where are you going to put the saltcellar?
B I'm going to put the saltcellar next to the side plate, on the right.

6 A drink?

The drinks menu

1 What do people usually drink before and during a restaurant meal?

Reading **2** Complete the Casablanca drinks menu with the words in the box.

> Hot drinks   Spirits   Teas   Soft drinks   Beers
> Coffees   Long drinks   Wines

DRINKS MENU

1 ....
- Cola
- Lemonade
- Mineral water
- Fruit juices

2 _Hot drinks_ ....

3 ....
- Espresso
- Cappuccino
- Irish coffee

4 ....
- Tea with lemon
- Camomile tea

5 ....
- Lager
- Bitter

6 ....
- House red
- House white
- Rosé
- Champagne

7 ....
- Brandy
- Cognac
- Whisky

8 ....
- Gin and tonic
- Cuba Libre
- Vodka and lemon

Casablanca

Speaking **3** Work in groups. How many drinks can you add to the menu?

Vocabulary

Describing drinks

4 Complete the diagram with the words in the box. Then practise saying the words.

sweet	sparkling	draught	still	herbal	
Irish coffee	dry	bottled	espresso	apple	fruit

canned

3 ....

beer

5 ....

2 ....

cappuccino

4 ....

wine

6 ....

coffees

1 ....

alcoholic

sparkling

HOT

DRINKS

COLD

teas

soft drinks

orange

10 ....

8 ....

mineral water

juices

11 ....

black

9 ....

7 ....

Listening

5 Listen to the waiter describing drinks. Which drinks is he talking about?

1 a) Irish coffee   b) camomile tea   c) whisky
2 a) gin and tonic   b) Cuba Libre   c) vodka and lemon
3 a) rosé   b) champagne   c) red wine
4 a) Irish coffee   b) espresso coffee   c) cappuccino
5 a) bitter   b) cognac   c) sherry
6 a) rosé   b) whisky   c) brandy

Speechwork

6 Which word has a different vowel sound?

1) wine	fine	tin	time
2) me	sweet	bread	tea
3) street	gin	drink	still
4) hot	map	hat	black
5) name	May	date	dry
6) floor	could	door	four
7) how	juice	two	you
8) waiter	table	lager	later

Now listen and check your answers. Then practise saying the words.

Vocabulary   Behind the bar

7 Match the words to the pictures. Use a dictionary to help you.

| eggs 8 sugar   salt   glasses   tomato juice   bottles   cocktail shakers   ice |

Which can be counted? Mark them as countable (C) or uncountable (U).

Language

Countable and uncountable nouns

- Countable nouns can be singular or plural and take *a / an* or a number.

  There **is a spoon** behind the bar.
  There **are five spoons** behind the bar.

- Uncountable nouns are never plural and cannot have *a / an* or a number.

  There **is** sugar behind the bar.

- Both countable and uncountable nouns use **some** or **any**.

  There **are some** eggs in the fridge.   **Are** there **any** glasses on the tray?
  There **is some** sugar in the pot.   There **isn't any** ketchup.

- Look at the sentences above and underline the correct options below.

  We use **some** with positive verbs / negative verbs / questions.
  We use **any** with positive verbs / negative verbs / questions.

▶ **Check your answers on page 96.**

Practice

8 Complete the description of the above picture with *some* or *any*.

There are ....some....¹ glasses and ....² bottles on the table, but there aren't
..................³ plates. There's ....⁴ salt, sugar and ice but there isn't ....⁵
pepper. There are ....⁶ eggs and there's ....⁷ tomato juice. There isn't
..................⁸ milk and there aren't ....⁹ napkins. There are ....¹⁰ cocktail
shakers, too.

Speaking

**9 Your teacher will stick the name of a drink on your back. Ask other students
Yes / No questions to find out the name of the drink.**

A: Is it an alcoholic drink?   B: No, it isn't.

Ordering a drink

1 Jan serves two guests. Listen and choose the correct answers for the questions below.

Jan	Would you like to order a drink?
Mr Kerrigan	Yes, could we see the wine list, please?
Jan	Certainly sir, here it is.
Mr Kerrigan	Thank you. I'll have a glass of dry white wine. And you, dear?
Mrs Kerrigan	Could I see the list, too, please?
Mr Kerrigan	Oh, yes, of course. Sorry.
Mrs Kerrigan	Thank you. There are some nice apéritifs. A sherry would be nice. No, I think a Martini. And could I have some ice in it, please?
Jan	Certainly madam. So, that's a dry white wine and a Martini with ice.
Mrs Kerrigan	Excuse me, could you close the window, please? It's a bit cold.
Jan	Certainly madam.
Mr Kerrigan	If you're cold, why do you want ice in your drink?

1 How many people are there in the conversation?
   a) two   b) three ✓   c) four
2 What does Mr Kerrigan ask to see?
   a) the menu   b) the bill   c) the wine list
3 What does Mr Kerrigan order?
   a) a beer   b) a glass of wine   c) a whisky
4 What kind of drink does Mrs Kerrigan order?
   a) a soft drink   b) an apéritif   c) a coffee
5 What drink does Mrs Kerrigan order?
   a) a Martini   b) a sherry   c) a gin and tonic
6 What does Mrs Kerrigan ask Jan to do?
   a) close a window   b) move the table   c) turn the heating up

6 A drink?

2 Listen to the conversation again and tick the sentences you hear.

1 Can you bring us a glass of water, please?
2 Could you bring us the wine list, please?
3 Could we see the wine list, please?
4 Could I see the list, too, please?
5 Could I have some ice in it, please?
6 Put some ice in it, please.
7 Could you close the window, please?
8 Close the window, it's a bit cold.

> **Culture tip**
>
> Politeness is always very important in English. Always remember to say **please** and **thank you**. When guests say *Thank you*, say **You're welcome**.

Practice

3 Put the words in the following sentences in the correct order.

1 you / Could / please / menu / bring / the / me
..*Could you bring me the menu, please?*..................

2 my / please / have / Can / coat / I
....

3 name / me / Could / your / tell / you / please
....

4 in / please / corner / we / a / Could / table / the / have
....

5 Peter / some / have / Can / I / bread
....

6 show / table / us / Could / please / you / our / to
....

Vocabulary

Tableware for drinks

4 Match the drinks to the pictures. What are the drinks in: *cups*, *mugs* or *glasses*?

| hot chocolate**3** cocktail beer wine coffee champagne tea |

Speechwork

5 **Listen to the pronunciation of *a* and *of* in these sentences. Then practise saying the sentences.**

Could I have a glass of wine, please?
Would you like a cup of coffee?

1 Could I have a glass of wine, please?
2 Would you like a cup of coffee?
3 There's a round table near the piano.
4 The bartender makes a special cocktail for me.
5 Is there a toilet here, please?
6 Is there a customer in the bar?
7 Would you like an apéritif, madam?
8 I'll have a pint of lager, please.

Vocabulary

Tableware for wine

6 **Match the words in the box to the pictures. Use a dictionary to help you.**

ice bucket **1**	decanter	wine label	wine basket
corkscrew	whitecloth	coaster	cork

Speaking

7 **Work in groups. One student be the waiter, the others be guests. Practise ordering drinks from the menu on page 40.**

8 **Work in groups. Your teacher will give you some playing cards and a set of questions. Each group takes a card and answers the appropriate question. If they give a correct answer they keep the card. If not, the other group tries to win the card. Add up the numbers on the cards and the group with the most points wins.**

7 Cocktails

After a long day

Speaking   1   What are your favourite cocktails? What ingredients are in them?

🎧 **Listening**   2   Rosa asks Peter to make her a cocktail. Listen and say whether the sentences below are true or false. Then correct the false sentences.

Rosa	Oh, what a day. I'm so tired!
Peter	How about a Spanish cocktail for a beautiful Spanish lady: a Mojito!
Rosa	Is that with rum?
Peter	It sure is. Rum, soda water, lime juice, sugar and a mint sprig.
Rosa	I'm sure it's delicious but it's not Spanish, it's Cuban. Anyway, I don't like rum.
Peter	OK, what about a Margarita then?
Rosa	I don't know. I think I'd prefer something non-alcoholic.
Peter	No problem. One non-alcoholic cocktail coming up! Right, try this.
Rosa	Hmm. This is great. What is it?
Peter	A San Francisco. You mix pineapple, orange and grapefruit juice. Then add grenadine and a splash of soda water and serve it.
Rosa	It sounds easy but how much of each ingredient do you need?
Peter	Don't worry, I can give you the recipe.
Rosa	That's great. I can make it for my friends. Thanks Peter.

1   Rosa is very tired.
2   The Mojito is a Spanish cocktail.
3   There is lime juice in the Mojito.
4   Rosa would like a soft drink.
5   The San Francisco has orange juice in it.
6   Rosa asks for the San Francisco recipe.

Vocabulary

Making cocktails

3 **Match the words in the box to the pictures. Then practise saying the words.**

salt **2**	mint leaves	grenadine	sugar
pineapple juice	ice	lime zest	grapefruit juice

4 **Read the dialogue again and complete the recipes.**

[COCKTAILS]

Mojito

3 tbsp of ....rum........[1], a splash of soda, a dash of lime ....[2], 1 tbsp of sugar, ...[3] sprig.

San Francisco

$^1/_3$ of pineapple ....[4], $^1/_3$ of orange juice $^1/_3$ of ....[5] juice, 2 dashes of grenadine, a splash of ....[6].

5 **Match the abbreviations to their full forms. Check your answers on page 91.**

1	tbsp	a)	teaspoon
2	g / gr	b)	tablespoon
3	l	c)	pound
4	cl	d)	ounce
5	kg	e)	gram
6	tsp	f)	litre
7	oz	g)	kilogram
8	lb	h)	centilitre

Culture tip

In the US ingredients are measured in spoons and cups. See the conversion table on page 91.

6 Which is the larger measure? Use the conversion table on page 91.

1 a) a dash	b) 3 fluid ounces ✓
2 a) a tablespoon	b) a teaspoon
3 a) a pound	b) an ounce
4 a) 2 tablespoons	b) a cup
5 a) a drop	b) a litre
6 a) a teaspoon	b) a cup
7 a) an ounce	b) a gram
8 a) a pound	b) a kilogram

Language

Imperatives

Look at these sentences and answer the questions.

a) Then **add** grenadine and a splash of soda water.

b) **Don't worry**, you can have the recipe.

c) You **mix** pineapple, orange and grapefruit juice.

- Which sentences are positive and which negative?
- Which sentences give instructions?
- Which sentences describe a process?
- Which sentence uses an imperative?

Imperatives do not have a subject before the verb and are used to give ....

▶ **Check your answers on page 96.**

Practice

7 Use the following information to give instructions.

1) to / list / take / the / table / wine / the
   <u>Take the wine list to the table.</u> ....

2) the / my / don't take / bag / cloakroom / to

   ....

3) some / bread / table / serve / to / two / more

   ....

4) number / guests / eight / table / don't show / the / to

   ....

5) for / cocktail / Mr Smith / a / prepare

   ....

6) the / fridge / in / don't put / milk / the

   ....

Who would normally say these sentences? Practise saying them.

Making cocktails

1 **Two guests are at the Casablanca bar. Listen and cross out the one incorrect answer from the options below.**

Mr Holland	And this is my favourite bar in London. Hello Peter, how are you?
Peter	Fine thanks, Mr Holland. What would you like to drink?
Mr Holland	Svetlana, this is Peter. You must try one of his cocktails.
Svetlana	OK. What do you recommend, Peter?
Peter	How about something British? A Gin Fizz? It's my favourite cocktail. It's made with gin, lemon juice, sugar and …
Svetlana	Sorry, I don't like gin very much. We don't drink it in Russia.
Peter	Ah, then perhaps something with vodka for the beautiful Russian lady? How about a Bloody Mary? Also very British, but with vodka.
Svetlana	What's in it?
Peter	Vodka, tomato juice, lemon juice, Tabasco and Worcestershire sauce.
Svetlana	OK. I'll have one of those.
Peter	Great! One Bloody Mary coming up. And for you Mr Holland? The usual?
Mr Holland	Yes please, Peter. A Gin Fizz is fine for me.

1 Mr Holland knows …
   a) London   b) the Casablanca   c) ~~Moscow~~
2 Peter recommends a …
   a) gin and tonic   b) Gin Fizz   c) Bloody Mary
3 Svetlana …
   a) doesn't drink alcohol   b) doesn't like gin   c) doesn't know the Casablanca
4 A Bloody Mary is made with …
   a) tomato juice   b) sugar   c) Worcestershire sauce
5 Gin Fizz is a favourite cocktail for …
   a) Peter   b) Mr Holland   c) Svetlana

Vocabulary   Cocktail preparation

2   You will receive two sets of cards: one with these words in English, one with them in your language. Put them face down on the table. Turn over one card from each set. If they are the same, keep them. If not, turn them over and let your partner try.

add	garnish	strain	serve	mix	shake
put	fill	stir	season	pour	

Speaking   3   Work in groups. One student acts one of the verbs of preparation. The other students say which verb it is.

Language   4   Look at the instructions for making a Bloody Mary. Underline the words which are used to put the instructions in a clear order.

Grammar

When we give instructions, we order them with words such as:
First,
Then,
Next,
Finally,

Bloody Mary

[COCKTAILS]

INGREDIENTS

3 tbsp vodka, 20 cl tomato juice, a dash of lemon juice, 2 or 3 drops of Worcestershire sauce, 2 or 3 drops Tabasco, pepper, salt, celery salt, celery stick

PREPARATION

First, put ice in a tall glass. Then add the Worcestershire sauce, the Tabasco, pepper, salt and celery salt. Next, fill the glass with the vodka and the tomato juice. Finally, stir and garnish with the celery stick.

Practice   5   Now use the words to complete the instructions for a Gin Fizz.

Gin Fizz

[COCKTAILS]

INGREDIENTS

3 tbsp gin, 1 tsp of sugar, the juice of half a lemon, a splash of soda, maraschino cherry, ice

PREPARATION

...............................[1], put ice in a tall glass. ....[2] add the gin and the sugar. ....[3] mix it with the juice of half a lemon and the soda. ....[4], serve it with a maraschino cherry.

6 Put the sentences in the correct order to complete the instructions.

Mojito   juice and the sugar. Then add the ice, the rum and a
splash / with a fresh mint sprig. / First, mix the mint / of soda. Finally,
garnish / leaves with a dash of lime

Margarita   garnish with lime zest. / with ice. Next, strain to serve in / First, mix
the tequila, the Cointreau and the / a salt-rimmed glass. Finally, / lime
juice. Shake

San Francisco   shaker and shake with ice. Then strain into / juices and the grenadine
into a cocktail / a sugar-rimmed glass. Don't add / First, pour all the / the
soda until the end.

Speaking

7 Work in groups. Create your own cocktail. Tell the class its name and what is in it.

🎧 **Speechwork**

Rhythm

**8 Say these pairs of sentences out loud with the marked pauses.
Which sound better? Listen and say which option you hear.**

1 a) First / mix the mint leaves.
    b) First mix the mint / leaves.

2 a) I really like it what / is it?
    b) I really like it / what is it?

3 a) Then add the / ice.
    b) Then / add the ice.

4 a) Relax / and let me prepare you a drink.
    b) Relax and let me prepare / you a drink.

5 a) I'm afraid / it's not Spanish it's Cuban.
    b) I'm afraid it's not Spanish / it's Cuban.

6 a) Finally / stir and garnish with lime zest.
    b) Finally stir and garnish / with lime zest.

Speaking

**9 Work in pairs. Use the information below to write a dialogue. Practise your
dialogue and then read it to the class.**

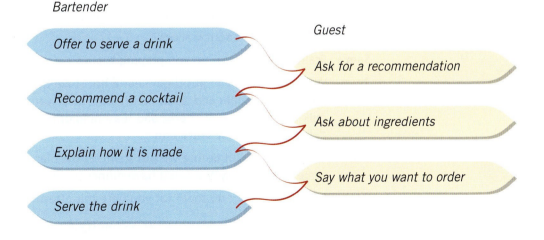

Bartender

Offer to serve a drink

Guest

Ask for a recommendation

Recommend a cocktail

Ask about ingredients

Explain how it is made

Say what you want to order

Serve the drink

8 Recipes

Changing the menu

1 Match the words in the box to the pictures. Use your dictionary to help you.

| oysters **5** | mussels | prawns | scallops | lobster |

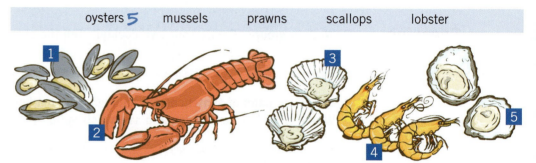

2 Listen to Rosa and Sam talk about the menu and put the sentences below into the correct order.

Sam   Rosa, I'd like to put a new seafood dish on the menu. Any suggestions?

Rosa   What about a prawn dish or mussels?

Sam   Well, mussels are the cheapest seafood and I think our guests have a more expensive taste than that.

Rosa   Yes, but their cheap price doesn't mean they taste worse than any other seafood. I think they're tastier than oysters, for example.

Sam   I agree, but I still don't think our customers will like mussels.

Rosa   Scallops. What about scallops?

Sam   Scallops, hmm. How do you prepare them?

Rosa   Well, first of all, you put them near a hot stove to open them up. Then you remove their shells and wash them under cold water and simmer them in a little milk with sliced onion, herbs and seasoning or in white wine stock. They're delicious in mornay sauce and …

Sam   Sounds great! But before we put them on the menu, why don't you prepare some for me to try. We could have dinner together at my place …

Rosa   It's OK Sam, I can do them for you here this afternoon.

- ☐ a) Sam and Rosa talk about prices and quality.
- ☐ 1 b) Sam asks for suggestions about changes to the menu.
- ☐ c) Rosa suggests another dish.
- ☐ d) Sam invites Rosa for dinner.
- ☐ e) Rosa suggests two dishes.
- ☐ f) Rosa explains how to cook scallops.

3 Answer the questions.

1 What kind of dish does Sam want to put on the menu?
2 Why are mussels not popular with the guests?
3 Which seafood do Sam and Rosa prefer to oysters?
4 Who knows how to prepare scallops?
5 When does Sam suggest they should try the scallops?
6 How does Rosa answer Sam?

Language

Comparatives and superlatives

Look at these sentences and complete the information below.

a) They're **cheaper than** oysters.
b) I think they're **tastier than** oysters.
c) Our guests have **more expensive** tastes.
d) Mussels are **the cheapest** seafood.
e) Lobster is **the most expensive** seafood on the menu.

	comparative form	superlative form
short adjectives	_-er_ + **than**	**the** + ...
adjectives ending -y	.... + ...	**the** + **-iest**
long adjectives	**more** + adjective	**the** + ... + ...

▶ **Check your answers on pages 96–97.**

Be careful of these irregular superlative and comparative forms:

good	→	better	→	the best
bad	→	**worse**	→	**the worst**

Practice

4 Use the information to write comparative and superlative sentences.

1 Prawns / tasty / oysters
   <u>Prawns are tastier than oysters.</u>

2 French wine / popular / in the UK
   ....

3 Milk / good / for you / lemonade
   ....

4 Lobster / expensive / seafood / on the menu
   ....

5 Champagne / good drink / in the world
   ....

6 Spaghetti carbonara / creamy / spaghetti Bolognese
   ....

7 Pasta / traditional / in Italy / in Spain
   ....

Grammar tip

Don't forget that comparatives are followed by *than*.

Vocabulary   Ingredients

5 Complete the diagram with the words in the box. Use a dictionary to help you.

seasoning   onion   fruit   dairy products   trout   parsley   flour   mussels
duck   lemon   prawns   potato   poultry   pork   cereal products

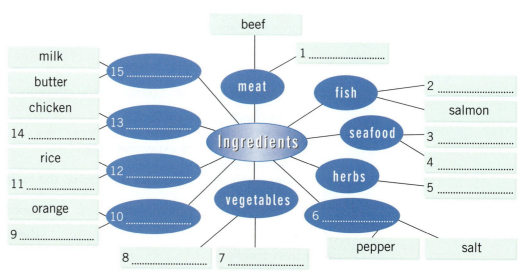

beef

milk
butter
chicken
14 ....
rice
11 ....
orange
9 ....

15 ....
13 ....
12 ....
10 ....

meat

Ingredients

vegetables

8 ....   7 ....

1 ....

fish

2 ....

salmon

seafood   3 ....

4 ....

herbs   5 ....

6 ....

pepper   salt

Think of two more words for each category. Use the glossary on pages 104–111.

Speaking   Describing restaurants

6 Use the words in the box to compare the three restaurants. Which restaurant would you like to go to? Why?

small   large   beautiful   old   traditional
comfortable   new   packed   cosy   modern

A seafood recipe

Reading

1 Complete the recipe from Rosa's cookery book with the words in the box.

Parmesan	cooked	pepper	potato	scallop
salamander	parsley	sauce		

Scallops in mornay sauce

Seafood

Ingredients

1 kg mashed potatoes
75 g butter
600 ml mornay sauce
20 cooked scallops
50 g grated Parmesan cheese
fresh parsley

Instructions

Prepare the mornay .... *sauce* ....[1]: take 500 ml hot béchamel, add 50 g butter, 100 ml cream and salt and ....[2]. Butter the ....[3] shells and decorate the edges with mashed ....[4]. Sprinkle with melted butter. Slice the ....[5] scallops. Pour a little of the mornay sauce into the bottom of the shells. Place the sliced scallops on top of the sauce. Cover with more mornay sauce. Sprinkle with grated ....[6] cheese and melted butter. Gratinate under a ....[7] grill. Serve with fresh ....[8].

Vocabulary

Verbs of preparation

2 Match the words in the box to the pictures. Then practise saying the words.

butter 8	grate	mash	marinate	pour	slice	sprinkle	pick

1   2   3   4

5   6   7   8

3 Match the verbs of preparation to the following.

1) butter	a) milk, water, wine
2) sprinkle	b) cheese, carrots
3) slice	c) potatoes
4) pour	d) butter, ice, chocolate
5) melt	e) grated cheese, herbs
6) mash	f) a cake tin, shells
7) pick	g) ham, cheese, a cake
8) grate	h) parsley, chives

4 Complete the sentences with the adjective form of the preparation verbs.

> **Grammar tip**
>
> By adding -ed to a preparation verb, it can also be used as an adjective:
>
> *If you **melt** butter, you get **melted** butter.*

1 Slice the (*cook*) ....cooked........ scallops and put them in the shells.

2 We serve (*gratinate*) .... macaroni for lunch.

3 Our (*grill*) .... salmon comes with (*mash*) .... potatoes and (*melt*) .... butter.

4 Beef carpaccio is (*slice*) .... beef with (*grate*) .... Parmesan cheese and freshly (*pick*) .... herbs.

5 Would you like your beef (*grill*) ...., (*bake*) .... or (*fry*) ....?

6 If you put (*melt*) .... chocolate over the (*slice*) .... pears, you get a lovely dessert.

7 There are (*grate*) .... carrots and freshly (*pick*) .... parsley on the salad.

🎧 **Speechwork**   *-ed* endings

5 Listen to the pronunciation of *-ed* at the end of these words.

*It comes with **mashed** potatoes.*
*I'll have the **grilled** salmon.*
*They're served with **melted** butter.*

Put the words into the correct groups.

gratinated	cooked	poured	picked	grated	sliced
fried	mashed	covered	sprinkled	buttered	marinated

/ɪd/	/d/ or /t/
gratinated	cooked

Now listen again and check your answers. Then practise saying the words.

6 **Work in groups. You are invited to prepare a traditional recipe from your country by a UK television channel. Plan your recipe and present it to the class.**

Remember to:

- introduce yourself (say who you are, where you are from)
- explain what you are going to prepare
- say where the dish comes from and why it is special
- list what you are going to use (ingredients, utensils)
- explain how to make the dish
- say goodbye

1 Complete the sentences with the correct form of *going to* + verb.

1 We (*have*) ......are going to have.... dinner with my parents on Sunday. We (*go*) .... to a new restaurant in the city centre.

2 (*order*) .... you .... fish or meat?

3 Next week Max (*work*) .... in the kitchen and you (*help*) .... the waiters in the dining-room.

4 The new bar in the High Street (*not open*) .... until next summer.

5 What (*do*) .... Chris .... on Monday? Isn't it his day off?

6 This evening the Head Chef (*cook*) .... a special meal, so I (*prepare*) .... all the ingredients in the afternoon.

7 When (*make*) .... you .... the booking, today or tomorrow?

8 The restaurant is fully booked tonight, so the waiters (*be*) .... very busy and they (*not finish*) .... before midnight.

2 Complete the dialogue with the correct options.

Amanda Are there (1) *some/ any* special arrangements this weekend, Judith?

Judith Yes, there are (2) *some/ any*. (3) The *more/ most* important one is a small wedding banquet on Sunday.

Amanda And where can we arrange it? In the private lounge?

Judith Well, the weather will probably be (4) *hotter/ more hot* than usual, so we could use the terrace.

Amanda The garden is (5) *more/ most* beautiful than the terrace. Why don't we do it there?

Judith Yes, you're right. And the garden is also (6) *larger/ more large* than the terrace. I'll inform the Manager right away. He knows (7) *any/ some* of the guests, so he wants to organise (8) the *better/ best* banquet for them. There will probably be (9) *some/ any* live music. Do you have (10) *any/ some* other suggestions?

3 Look at the mixed-up recipes for Beef Stroganoff and Gin Daiquiri. Complete the instructions with the words in the box.

cut	strain	shake	boil	fry	fill	season

1) First, ...cut.......... the meat into pieces and season it.

2) Cook the chopped onions in the same butter you used for the meat.

3) .... the drink into a glass filled with ice.

4) Finally, ... and serve.

5) Then .... the pieces of beef in butter, keeping them underdone.

6) Remove and retain the slightly fried meat in a warm place.

7) Finally, garnish with a lime slice.

8) Add the fried meat and the lemon juice to the onions.

9) Next, add the gin, the rum, the lime juice and the sugar and ....

10) Add the cream to the onions, ... and reduce by half.

11) First, ... a shaker with ice.

Now put the instructions in the correct order.

Beef Stroganoff

.... 1

....

....

....

....

....

Gin Daiquiri

....

....

....

....

....

4 Put the words in the box in the correct groups.

> add, centilitre, coffee pot, cork, dairy products, dance floor, decanter, fruit, garnish, juice, label, lemonade, mineral water, napkin, non-smoking section, poultry, saucer, slipcloth, stir, sugar bowl, tablecloth, tablespoon, teaspoon, terrace

Wine	Restaurant sections	Tableware	Soft drinks

Verbs of preparation	Measures	Tea and coffee	Food

5 Look at the pictures below and work in four groups. Group 1: You are a group of friends who want to celebrate a birthday at a bar. Think about how you want to celebrate it (drinks, music, atmosphere). Groups 2–4: You each work in one of the bars below. Think about what you are going to offer the guests and what makes your bar better than the other two.

When you are ready, the three bars each present their ideas to the guests. The guests then decide which bar is best for their birthday party.

9

Here's the menu

The menu

Speaking 1 What can you find on an à la carte menu? How is it organised?

Reading 2 Complete the Casablanca à la carte menu with the words in the box.

side dishes	cold	vegetarian dishes	starters
meat dishes	hot	fish dishes	main courses

MENU

1 Starters

2 ....

- Avocado pear with Mediterranean prawns.
- Norwegian salmon carpaccio.
- Goose pâté with rosemary.
- Vichyssoise.

3 ....

- Warm salad with goat's cheese and crispy bacon.
- French onion soup with grated Parmesan cheese.
- Home-made chicken and mushroom croquettes.
- Polish potato pancakes.

4 ....

5 ....

- Roast beef with assorted vegetables.
- Veal cutlets with grilled tomatoes.
- Sirloin steak with broccoli and apple sauce.
- Casablanca couscous with lamb.

6 ....

- Sole meunière with jacket potatoes.
- North Sea eel with lobster sauce.
- Scallops in mornay sauce.
- Fresh seafood paella.

7 ....

- Green lasagne with three-cheese sauce.
- Sautéed mushrooms and bamboo with soy sauce.

8 ....

- Your choice of salads: Waldorf, Caesar, Greek, Casablanca Special.
- Your choice of potatoes: fried, grilled, jacket, boiled.

Casablanca

How is the menu different to ones in your country?

Vocabulary　Starters and main courses

3 Match the words in the box to the pictures. Then practise saying the words.

| avocado pear **2**　goose　　rosemary　　goat　　potato　　beef　　veal |
| cutlet　　sirloin steak　　broccoli　　eel　　sole　　lobster　　lamb |

Dishes

4 Match the dishes to the descriptions.

1) carpaccio	a) traditional Spanish rice dish
2) couscous	b) thin slices of raw fish or meat
3) pâté	c) smooth, soft mixture of meat, fish or vegetables that can be spread on bread
4) salad	d) cold starter or side dish of mainly raw vegetables
5) croquette	e) flat, round mixture of several ingredients fried in a pan
6) pancake	f) traditional North African cereal dish
7) paella	g) traditional Italian pasta dish
8) lasagne	h) mashed vegetables, meat or fish coated with breadcrumbs and deep-fried

5 Look at the following words describing dishes. What do they describe?

(a) Where the dish / ingredient comes from　　(c) How it is prepared
(b) Which animal or vegetable is used

1) Mediterranean _a_	8) soya	15) onion ....
2) Polish	9) grated	16) mushroom ....
3) North Sea	10) French	17) potato ....
4) salmon	11) lobster	18) grilled ....
5) goose	12) goat	19) jacket ....
6) veal	13) seafood	20) sautéed ....
7) boiled	14) roast	

6 **Put these words in order to get names of dishes.**

1) pea / Dutch / soup ...... Dutch pea soup ......

2) stew / Spanish / pork ....

3) lemon / grilled / sauce / cod / with ....

4) mushrooms / with / roast / sautéed / duck ....

5) caviare / Russian / fresh ....

6) jacket / lamb / with / Scottish / potatoes ....

Language

Past simple (regular verbs)

Look at these sentences and answer the questions below.

Alice   *I **loved** the dinner party last night.*
Maria   *Yes, me too. **Did** Woody **eat** the chocolate cake?*
Alice   *No, he **didn't have** any of it. He **doesn't like** chocolate. But I love it!*

- What's the difference between **loved** and **love**?
- What is the past form of **do / does**?
- Can you use an **-ed** verb after **did**?

▶ **Check your answers on page 97.**

- We use the past simple to refer to past actions.
- We add **-ed** to verbs to form the past simple. Some verbs do not follow this rule (see pages 97–98).
- To form negatives and questions, we use **did** + the infinitive form of the verb.

Practice

7 **Complete the sentences with the correct form of the past simple.**

1 Rosa and Jan (*start*) ...... started ...... to work in the restaurant around October.

2 Susan (*introduce*) .... Jan to Mr Grant on his first day at work.

3 Sam (*not / introduce*) .... Rosa to the Hotel Manager, but to the rest of the kitchen staff.

4 Ms Georgina Porter (*book*) .... her wedding banquet at the Casablanca.

5 (*show*) .... Jan .... the American guest the way to the Casablanca?

6 Jan was very nervous when he (*fill*) .... in his first booking form.

7 Jan also (*welcome*) .... the Kerrigans to the restaurant, but he (*not / present*) .... them with the menu.

8 (*like*) .... Rosa .... the cocktail Peter (*prepare*) .... for her?

Speaking

8 **Work in pairs. Student A turn to page 89. Student B use the verbs in the box to find out what your partner did last week.**

| watch | work | study | buy | go | prepare |

A: Did you watch any films last week?   B: Yes, I watched a film with Mel Gibson.

Are you ready to order?

1 **Listen to Jan take an order and complete the table below.**

Jan	Are you ready to order?	
Alison	Not really. Could you tell me what carpaccio is?	
Jan	Of course madam. It's made of marinated salmon slices served with toast.	
Alison	I see. And what's vichyssoise?	
Jan	Vichyssoise is made of potato, celery and onion. It's served as a cold soup.	
Fiona	That sounds nice. I think I'll have that for a starter.	
Alison	I feel like a hot starter. Do the Polish potato pancakes have garlic in them?	
Jan	No, madam.	
Alison	Good, I'll have that then.	
Jan	And what would you like as a main course?	
Fiona	I think I'll go for the Casablanca couscous.	
Jan	So couscous for you madam. And for you, madam?	
Alison	Let me see. The North Sea eel looks delicious. I think I'll have that.	
Jan	Excellent choice madam. Would you like a side dish to go with it?	
Alison	OK, we'll share a Waldorf salad.	
Jan	A Waldorf salad. And what would you like to drink?	
Alison	We'll have a bottle of house rosé, please.	
Jan	Certainly madam. Thank you.	

	Alison	Fiona
Starter	Polish potato pancakes	
Main course		
Side dish		
Drinks		

Language

Taking orders

2 Now read the dialogue and find the phrases Jan uses to do the following.

1) make sure the guests are ready to order .... *Are you ready to order?* ....

2) say OK in a formal way ....

3) ask for the guest's choice of main course ....

4) confirm the guest's choice ....

5) ask for the next guest's choice ....

6) praise the guest's choice ....

7) ask if a side dish is required ....

8) ask for the guest's choice of drinks ....

9) end the order ....

Practice

3 Find one wrong word in each sentence and correct it.

1 Are you ready to (book?)

.... *Are you ready to order?* ....

2 What would you want as a main course?

....

3 And for the madam?

....

4 Very bad choice, sir.

....

5 Would you like a dessert to go with the steak?

....

6 What do you like to drink?

....

🎧 Speechwork

Pronouncing French words

4 Listen to these French words pronounced by a French person or by an English person. Who says each word? Write F (French) or E (English).

¹ pâté

² vichyssoise

³ mornay

⁴ meunière

⁵ croquette

⁶ sommelier

⁷ sautéed

⁸ rosé

Now listen to the correct pronunciations and practise saying the words.

Language

Describing dishes

5 Look at this sentence and the information in the box. Complete the box with carpaccio and another dish from the dialogue on page 63.

Name of dish	is made of	how the raw ingredients are prepared	ingredients	(served) with	what complements the raw materials
It				and it's served as	kind of dish

Name of dish	is made of	how the raw ingredients are prepared	ingredients	(served) with	what complements the raw materials
1 Carpaccio	is made of	marinated	salmon	served with	toast.
2					

Practice

6 Now use the information to describe the following dishes.

1 Scallops in mornay sauce
   It's made of boiled scallops served with mornay sauce. The mornay sauce is made of béchamel, butter, cream, salt and pepper.

2 Green lasagne with three-cheese sauce

3 Fresh seafood paella

4 Casablanca couscous with lamb

5 Polish potato pancakes

6 Warm salad with goat's cheese and crispy bacon

7 Work in groups. Design a menu for your own restaurant. Then work with someone from another group. Practise ordering dishes and taking note of the orders.

10 The chef recommends

Desserts

Speaking **1** What type of dessert is traditional in your country? What is it made of?

🎧 Listening **2** Listen to two guests order dessert and complete the table opposite.

Thomas	And now my favourite part: desserts! Excuse me, what's sachertorte?
Jan	Sachertorte? It's an Austrian chocolate cake served with hot chocolate sir. If you like chocolate you should try it.
Thomas	Sounds great, I'll have that.
Mary	And I'd like something lighter. What do you recommend?
Jan	I would suggest our raspberry sorbet or the lemon mousse. Both are refreshing and light.
Mary	Maybe the raspberry sorbet if it's not too sweet.
Jan	I can also recommend the tiramisu.
Mary	What's that?
Jan	It's an Italian speciality made with coffee, amaretto and mascarpone cheese.
Thomas	That sounds good, I think I'll change my mind. I'll have that.
Jan	Very well, sir.
Mary	Nothing for me. I can have a bit of your tiramisu Thomas, can't I?

	Mary	Thomas	Jan
1 Who knows what sachertorte is?			✓
2 Who chooses a chocolate dessert?			
3 Who asks for a light dessert?			
4 Who doesn't want a very sweet dish?			
5 Who recommends something Italian?			
6 Who changes the order?			

Language

Recommending dishes

Look at this sentence and the information in the box.

If you like chocolate, you should try the chocolate mousse.

If you	like	soup cheese chocolate	I (would) suggest (you try)	the onion soup. the cheese sauce.
			I (can) recommend	the chocolate mousse.
	feel like	something different	you should try	the tiramisu.

Practice

3 Complete the recommendations with the words in the box.

> feel like   would   recommend   try   should   would suggest   should try

1 If you .... a filling dish, you .... try the Polish potato pancakes.

2 I can .... the sautéed mushrooms and bamboo with soy sauce.

3 If you like exotic dishes, I .... suggest the avocado pear with prawns.

4 If you like seafood, you .... the fresh seafood paella.

5 I .... you .... our Waldorf salad.

Speechwork

4 Listen to these recommendations. Mark each sentence as enthusiastic (E) or unenthusiastic (U).

1 Today's special is the fabulous pizza Napoli.
2 If you feel like a sweet dessert you should try the chocolate cake.
3 I would recommend the onion soup. I'm sure you'll find it delicious, madam.
4 Today the chef recommends the seafood paella. It's our speciality.
5 If you like cheese, you should try the green lasagne with the three-cheese sauce.
6 May I suggest this white Bourgogne? It's perfect with fish.

Now underline the words which are stressed in the enthusiastic sentences. Then correct the unenthusiastic sentences and practise saying them.

Speaking

5 Work in pairs. Use the phrases to recommend restaurants.

If you like Italian food, you should try Gino's.

Vocabulary

2 Read the dialogue again and complete the recipe for tiramisu.

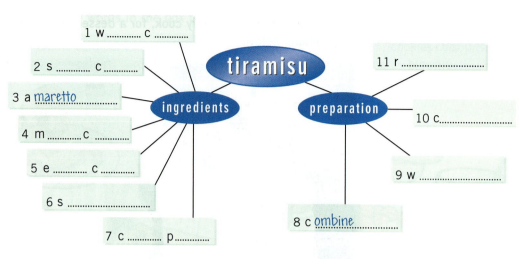

1 w .... c ....

2 s .... c ....

3 a maretto

4 m .... c ....

5 e .... c ....

6 s ....

7 c .... p ....

ingredients

tiramisu

preparation

11 r ....

10 c...........................

9 w ....

8 c ombine

Speaking

3 Work in pairs. Close your books and tell your partner how to make tiramisu.

Language

Past simple (irregular verbs)

Look at these sentences and the information below.

Jan   Some customers **had** tiramisu last night.
Louis   And what **did** they **think**? Did they like it?
Jan   They **said** it **was** delicious and they **didn't leave** any.

• These verbs are irregular because they never take **-ed** in the past.
• With negative sentences and questions use **did** and an infinitive.
• The past form of the verb **be** is **was** (I, he, she, it) or **were** (you, we, they).
• The verb **be** does not use **did** for negative sentences and questions.

▶ **For information see page 98.**

Practice

4 Complete the dialogue with the correct form of the past simple.

Louis   So, how (go) ..did..¹ the dinner ..go.. yesterday?

Jan   Don't ask! It (be) ....² a disaster!

Louis   (have) .... you ....³ problems with the tiramisu?

Jan   No, not exactly. I (have) ....⁴ two guests instead of one.

Louis   What?

Jan   Rosa (bring) ....⁵ someone with her!

Louis   No! Who (be) ....⁶ it?

Jan   Susan, the Head Waiter! There I (be) ....⁷, all ready for a romantic dinner. I

        (put) ....⁸ candles and flowers on the table and (choose) ....⁹ Spanish music

        for the perfect atmosphere. And then the bell (ring) ....¹⁰ and there

        (be) ....¹¹ the two of them: Rosa and my boss!

Louis   But what (be) ....¹² the tiramisu like?

Jan   I (not / try) ....¹³ any because I only (make) ....¹⁴ enough for two people.

        But they (say) ....¹⁵ it (be) ....¹⁶ delicious.

Louis   So, what's the problem? Your dinner (be) ____¹⁷ a success!

A dessert recipe

🎧 Listening

1 Jan asks Louis, the pastry cook, for a dessert recipe. Listen and answer the questions below.

Jan	Louis, could you give me the recipe for a simple dessert? Something that's easy to prepare. It's for a dinner.
Louis	What about a tiramisu?
Jan	Tiramisu? Some customers had that last night.
Louis	And what did they think? Did they like it?
Jan	They said it was delicious and they didn't leave any. Is it easy to prepare?
Louis	Yeah. I can give you a simple recipe using American measuring cups. How many is the dinner for?
Jan	Just for two.
Louis	Oh, I see. Well, you'll need mascarpone cheese, whipping cream, sugar, amaretto, espresso, sponge-cake and cocoa powder. Combine the mascarpone cheese, the cream, the sugar, the amaretto and the espresso in a large bowl and then whip it all until it thickens.
Jan	What about the sponge-cake?
Louis	Put it at the bottom of the mould and then cover it with the cream mixture. Finally, you put another layer of sponge-cake on top. Then refrigerate for one hour and serve with cocoa powder on top. Does Rosa like tiramisu?
Jan	I hope so. How did you know it was Rosa?

1 Who is planning a romantic dinner?
2 Who suggests a dessert recipe?
3 What's the dessert?
4 How many ingredients do you need to prepare the dessert?
5 How many guests are invited?

Vocabulary 2 **Read the dialogue again and complete the recipe for tiramisu.**

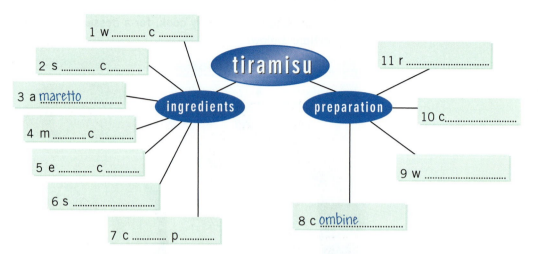

1 w .... c ....

2 s .... c ....

3 a maretto ....

4 m .... c ....

5 e .... c ....

6 s ....

7 c .... p ....

tiramisu

ingredients

preparation

11 r ....

10 c ....

9 w ....

8 c ombine ....

Speaking 3 **Work in pairs. Close your books and tell your partner how to make tiramisu.**

Language

Past simple (irregular verbs)

Look at these sentences and the information below.

Jan   *Some customers **had** tiramisu last night.*
Louis   *And what **did** they **think**? Did they like it?*
Jan   *They **said** it **was** delicious and they **didn't leave** any.*

- These verbs are irregular because they never take **-ed** in the past.
- With negative sentences and questions use **did** and an infinitive.
- The past form of the verb **be** is **was** (I, he, she, it) or **were** (you, we, they).
- The verb **be** does not use **did** for negative sentences and questions.

▶ **For information see page 98.**

Practice 4 **Complete the dialogue with the correct form of the past simple.**

Louis   So, how (go) ..did..¹ the dinner ..go.. yesterday?

Jan   Don't ask! It (be) ....² a disaster!

Louis   (have) .... you ....³ problems with the tiramisu?

Jan   No, not exactly. I (have) ....⁴ two guests instead of one.

Louis   What?

Jan   Rosa (bring) ....⁵ someone with her!

Louis   No! Who (be) ....⁶ it?

Jan   Susan, the Head Waiter! There I (be) ....⁷, all ready for a romantic dinner. I

(put) ....⁸ candles and flowers on the table and (choose) ....⁹ Spanish music

for the perfect atmosphere. And then the bell (ring) ....¹⁰ and there

(be) ....¹¹ the two of them: Rosa and my boss!

Louis   But what (be) ....¹² the tiramisu like?

Jan   I (not / try) ....¹³ any because I only (make) ....¹⁴ enough for two people.

But they (say) ....¹⁵ it (be) ....¹⁶ delicious.

Louis   So, what's the problem? Your dinner (be) ____¹⁷ a success!

	Mary	Thomas	Jan
1 Who knows what sachertorte is?			✓
2 Who chooses a chocolate dessert?			
3 Who asks for a light dessert?			
4 Who doesn't want a very sweet dish?			
5 Who recommends something Italian?			
6 Who changes the order?			

Language

Recommending dishes

Look at this sentence and the information in the box.

If you like chocolate, you should try the chocolate mousse.

If you	like	soup cheese chocolate	I (would) suggest (you try)	the onion soup. the cheese sauce.
			I (can) recommend	the chocolate mousse.
	feel like	something different	you should try	the tiramisu.

Practice

3 Complete the recommendations with the words in the box.

| feel like   would   recommend   try   should   would suggest   should try |

1 If you .... a filling dish, you .... try the Polish potato pancakes.

2 I can .... the sautéed mushrooms and bamboo with soy sauce.

3 If you like exotic dishes, I .... suggest the avocado pear with prawns.

4 If you like seafood, you .... the fresh seafood paella.

5 I .... you .... our Waldorf salad.

Speechwork

4 Listen to these recommendations. Mark each sentence as enthusiastic (E) or unenthusiastic (U).

1 Today's special is the fabulous pizza Napoli.
2 If you feel like a sweet dessert you should try the chocolate cake.
3 I would recommend the onion soup. I'm sure you'll find it delicious, madam.
4 Today the chef recommends the seafood paella. It's our speciality.
5 If you like cheese, you should try the green lasagne with the three-cheese sauce.
6 May I suggest this white Bourgogne? It's perfect with fish.

Now underline the words which are stressed in the enthusiastic sentences. Then correct the unenthusiastic sentences and practise saying them.

Speaking

5 Work in pairs. Use the phrases to recommend restaurants.

If you like Italian food, you should try Gino's.

Vocabulary   Desserts

6 Match the words in the box to the picture. Then practise saying the words.

| crème caramel **1**   sorbet   mousse   ice cream   cake   cookies / biscuits |
| yoghurt   milk shake   apple pie   pancake / crêpe   brownie |
| trifle   jelly   cheese   fruit salad |

Listening   **7 Listen to the guests. Which dessert would Jan recommend to each guest?**

1 a) yoghurt   b) pancakes   c) chocolate cake
2 a) brownies   b) milk shake   c) cookies
3 a) strawberry ice cream b) nougat ice cream c) pistachio ice cream
4 a) crème caramel   b) cheese   c) strawberry mousse
5 a) nuts   b) lemon sorbet   c) trifle
6 a) vanilla ice cream   b) coffee ice cream c) chocolate ice cream

Speaking   **8 Work in pairs. Use the information to write a dialogue. Practise your dialogue and then read it to the class.**

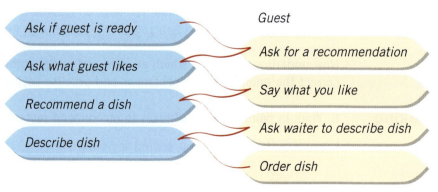

Waiter

Ask if guest is ready

Ask what guest likes

Recommend a dish

Describe dish

Guest

Ask for a recommendation

Say what you like

Ask waiter to describe dish

Order dish

Vocabulary

Utensils

5 Match the words in the box to the pictures. Then practise saying the words.

| bowl **7** | mould | wire whisk | wooden spoon | grater | frying pan | saucepan |
| skimmer | ladle | colander | baking tin | scissors | chef's knife | potato peeler |

Verbs of preparation

6 Match the words in the box to the pictures. Then practise saying the words.

| stir **9** | peel | cut | strain | bake | whip | grate | serve | skim | mix |

Now match the verbs of preparation to the utensils.

7 Work in groups. Prepare a dessert recipe and then read it to the rest of the class. The rest of the class take notes. Include the following information.

- ingredients for the recipe
- the necessary utensils
- step-by-step instructions

11 Complaints

Making a complaint

Speaking   **1** What do guests complain about in restaurants?

🎧 **Listening**   **2** Listen to five complaints and match them to the pictures.

3 Listen to the guests again and make a note of what each complaint is about.

Complaint
Guest 1 (.e.) ordered scallops – got sole
Guest 2 (.....)
Guest 3 (.....)
Guest 4 (.....)
Guest 5 (.....)

Vocabulary   Complaints about food

4 Match the adjectives to the pictures. Cross out any which don't match.

well-done   stale
cold   hot
hard

spicy
~~medium~~
dry
cold
hot

corked
stale
spongy
salty
sweet

tough   overcooked   underdone
rare   sweet

Language   5 Match the complaints to the types of food.

	too spicy	not warm enough	undercooked	stale
cutlets		✓	✓	
paella				
sole				
chicken				
rolls				

Present perfect

Look at these sentences and the information below.

*We've already **ordered**.*
*We **haven't ordered** yet.*
***Have** you **ordered** yet?*

- We make the present perfect of regular verbs with **have/has** + the **-ed** form.
- We make the present perfect of irregular verbs with **have/has** + the 3rd form of the verb (see page 99).
- We make negative sentences of regular verbs with **haven't/hasn't** + the **-ed** form or the 3rd form of irregular verbs.
- We make questions with **Have/Has** + the person + the **-ed** or 3rd form of the verb.
- We use the present perfect to talk about things we have or haven't done.

▶ **For more information see pages 98–99.**

Practice

6 **Karl, the commis, helps Sam in the kitchen. Look at his list of jobs and complete the dialogue.**

> • *boil potatoes* ✔   • *slice ham* ✔
> • *grate Parmesan cheese* ✔   • *marinate salmon*
> • *peel tomatoes*   • *dice carrots*
> • *chop onions* ✔   • *give menu to Susan* ✔

Sam   Karl, ...*have you boiled*.... [1] the potatoes?

Karl Yes, I have. And I .... [2] the Parmesan.

Sam   What about the tomatoes? .... [3] them yet?

Karl No, I .... [4] the tomatoes yet. But I .... [5] the onions and I .... [6] the ham.

Sam   Good. .... [7] the salmon?

Karl No, I .... [8]. I .... [9] the carrots yet but I .... [10] the menu to Susan already.

Speaking

7 **Work in pairs. Student B turn to page 87. Student A find out from your partner which of the following jobs Karl has done. Then look at the picture below and answer your partner's questions.**

Karl
• *empty rubbish*
• *clean oven*
• *take fruit out of the fridge*
• *clean wine glasses*
• *put pans away*
• *bake rolls for dinner*

Dealing with complaints

🎧 **Listening**

1 **Listen to a guest complain and answer the questions.**

Jan	I'm very sorry sir.
Guest	Look what you've done! My new suit is covered in cheese sauce!
Jan	I do apologise sir. Let me try to clean it for you.
Guest	No. This is a very expensive suit. I want to speak to the manager.
Jan	Certainly sir. I'll ask her to come as soon as possible.
Susan	Good evening sir. My name's Susan Davies. I'm the Head Waiter. What's the problem?
Guest	The problem is your waiter has spilled sauce all over me! Look at my new suit. It's covered in cheese sauce.
Susan	Please accept my apologies.
Guest	But what about my suit?
Susan	We'll pay for it to be cleaned, of course, but could I try to clean it for you with water first? Could we offer you a coffee while you wait? It's on the house.
Guest	All right then. I'll have a large cappuccino with chocolate on top and a biscuit.

1 What does Jan spill on the guest?
2 What does Jan do first?
3 Why does the guest want to see the manager?
4 What does Susan do?
5 Who pays for the coffee?

2 Listen again and complete the sentences.

1 I do .... *apologise* .... sir.

2 Let me .... it for you.

3 I want to .... the manager.

4 Certainly sir. I'll ask him to come ....

5 I'm the Head Waiter. What .... ?

6 Please accept ....

7 We'll pay for it .... , of course.

8 Could I try .... it for you with water first?

9 Could we .... a coffee while you wait?

10 It's on ....

Language

3 Susan gives Jan some advice on dealing with complaints. Match the tips to the sentences below.

> **1** *ask what the problem is*
>
> **2** *apologise*
>
> **3** *explain the reason for*
> *the problem*
>
> **4** *offer a solution*
> *or compensation*

a) Please accept my apologies. 2
b) I do apologise sir.
c) I'll ask the manager to come.
d) What is the problem?
e) There aren't any more tables available.
f) I'll ask the chef to heat it up for you.
g) I'm afraid we're very busy this evening.
h) Could we offer you a coffee on the house?
i) I'm very sorry sir.
j) We'll pay for it to be cleaned.

Now listen to check your answers. Then practise saying the sentences politely.

Practice

4 Put the following dialogue in the correct order.

☐ a) **Guest** We'd appreciate that. Thank you. And, another thing, this glass is dirty. There's lipstick on it!

☐ b) **Waiter** Yes, madam. How can I help you?

☐ c) **Guest** Thank you.

☐ d) **Waiter** I'm terribly sorry, madam. I'll bring a clean one immediately.

☐ e) **Guest** We ordered our food forty minutes ago.

☐ f) **Waiter** I apologise, madam. I'm afraid we're very busy and we're short-staffed. I'll see to it personally that you're served as soon as possible.

☐1 g) **Guest** Waiter, please!

Now listen and check your answers. Then practise the dialogue.

Speechwork

5 **Listen to the different pronunciations of these words. The first one is UK English and the second is US English.**

| water | can't | waiter | half | forty | dance | bottle | tomato |

Now listen to these sentences and write US if you hear US English and UK if you hear UK English.

1 We ordered sparkling water, not still.
2 This tomato soup is cold.
3 We can't dance here. The music is awful!
4 Could we have another bottle of wine? This one's corked.
5 I'm afraid we can't seat forty people, madam.
6 The waiter isn't very friendly, is he?
7 We can't talk here – the music's too loud.
8 We ordered our food over half an hour ago.

Vocabulary

Complaints

6 **Complete the complaints with the words in the box. Use a dictionary to help you.**

| missing | busy | blunt | dirty | cracked | noisy | rude | slow | broken | draughty |

1 I'm sorry about the service this evening but we're very ....busy........... .
2 Could you close the window, please? It's a bit .... here.
3 I can't cut my steak with this knife. It's ....
4 They haven't cleaned this place for years. It's so ....
5 The service in this restaurant is so .... We ordered over an hour ago.
6 Be careful! The glass is .... and there are pieces everywhere!
7 Waiter, could you change my cup? It's .... and I nearly cut my lip.
8 How can I eat my soup? My soup spoon is ....
9 This restaurant is very .... The music is too loud.
10 The waiter's so .... He's not polite at all.

Speaking

7 **Work in pairs. Use one word from each of the discs below to produce a dialogue. Throw a dice or spin each disc to find out which words to use.**

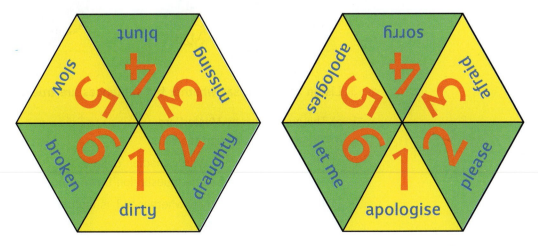

12 The bill, please

Asking for the bill

Speaking

1 How many currencies do you know? Which are the most common foreign currencies used by visitors to your country?

🎧 **Listening**

2 Listen to the three guests and match them to the correct pictures.

Culture tip

How much do restaurant guests usually tip in your country? Is service usually included in the bill?

3 Listen again and say whether the sentences are true or false.

1 a) The guest pays by MasterCard.
   b) The waiter has to sign the bill.
2 a) The guest wants to pay in Canadian dollars.
   b) Service is included so the guests don't give a tip.
3 a) The guest wants to know whether VAT is included.
   b) The guest leaves a tip.

Vocabulary

Methods of payment

4 Match the words in the box to the pictures.

| credit card **3** | coins | traveller's cheques | bank notes |

5 Complete the sentences with *in* or *by*.

1 Can I pay ......*by*.... credit card?

2 I'll ask the cashier to prepare the bill .... dollars.

3 That's great. I'll pay .... Visa.

4 Can we pay .... traveller's cheque?

5 I prefer to pay .... cash, if that's OK.

6 How will you be paying sir? .... cash or .... credit card?

Currencies

6 Match the words in the box to the pictures. What are the countries?

| peso | US dollar | Euro | cruzeiro | rouble | pound sterling | yen | Australian dollar |

7 Look at the nouns in the table below. Are they countable or uncountable?

	countable	uncountable
1 money		✓
2 dollars		
3 work		
4 waiters		
5 guests		

positive	negative	question	quantifier
✓			a lot of

Now look at these sentences and complete the rest of the table.

1 That's a lot of money.
2 There aren't many dollars on the table.
3 Is there much work in the kitchen?
4 There isn't much money in the cash desk.
5 Are there many waiters in the Casablanca?
6 There are a lot of guests in the dining-room.

Language

Much / many / a lot of

Look at these sentences and complete the information below.

*There are **a lot of** drinks on the bill.*   *That's **a lot of** VAT.*
*There aren't **many** waiters here.*   *We don't have **much** wine left.*
*How **many** starters did we have?*   *How **much** is the bill?*

- We use *a lot of* with ....uncountable........ and ....
  nouns in positive sentences.

- We use *many* with .... nouns in .... sentences
  and ....

- We use *much* with .... nouns in ....
  sentences and ....

▶ **Check your answers on page 99.**

8 Complete the sentences with the correct options.

1 A Are there *much / many* new dishes on the menu?
  B Yes, there are *a lot of / much* new starters.
2 A There's too *much / many* noise in this room.
  B Yes, there are *a lot of / much* people in here.
3 A There are too *much / many* desserts on this bill.
  B You're right. And there's *a lot of / much* tax as well.
4 A How *much / many* was the wine?
  B I'm not sure. How *much / many* glasses did we have?
5 A I think there are *a lot of / much* mistakes on this bill.
  B I think you're right. We didn't spend that *much / many* money.
6 A The service is slow. There aren't *many / much* waiters here.
  B I know. All the waiters have *a lot of / much* tables to serve.

Explaining the bill

🎧 **Listening**

1 Three guests ask Jan for the bill. Listen and say whether the sentences are true or false.

1 The guests ordered from the à la carte menu.
2 Drinks are included in the table d'hôte menu.
3 The guests knew that VAT was part of the bill.
4 The guests are from France.
5 Rosa knows the guests.

2 Listen again and complete the bill.

```
                       ✳ ✳ ✳

6 October


Table d'hôte menu        × 3                  ¹ £60 ............

Apéritifs                × ² .............     £10.50

Spirits                  × ³ .............     £9.00

Bottle of house wine     × 1                  ⁴ ............

                         Subtotal:            ⁵ ............

                         VAT & service:       £29.61


                         Total:               ⁶ ............


Thank you for your visit.                     Casablanca

                                  5 Hanover Street London WIA 4BZ
```

Vocabulary   Calculating figures

3 Put the words in the box in the correct groups. Use a dictionary to help you.

plus	equals	multiplied by	divided by	take away
minus		add on	makes	times

+	−	×	÷	=
plus				

Figures

Look at these sentences and the information below.

The new tableware cost $1,200. (one thousand two hundred dollars)
The bill comes to £24.80. (twenty-four pounds eighty)

- In English a comma shows thousands.
- A point shows decimals (but is not spoken).
- The currency is spoken after the number but before any decimals.

Practice   **4 Write the following sums in numbers and calculate the answers.**

1 One hundred and eight plus two point five. $108 + 2.5 = 110.5$

2 One thousand six hundred minus two hundred and four.   _____

3 Four hundred and forty-seven multiplied by two.   _____

4 Five hundred and fifty plus sixty-three.   _____

5 Sixty-nine divided by three.   _____

6 Seven hundred and fifty-seven minus eighty-nine.   _____

7 Five times nineteen.   _____

8 Nine thousand nine hundred and ninety-nine plus one.   _____

9 Two and a half plus one hundred and seven.   _____

10 Seven point three five minus one point two one.   _____

🎧 **Now listen and check your answers.**

5 Use a newspaper currency table to calculate these figures in your own currency.

your currency

1) £50   _____

2) $50   _____

3) £22,000   _____

4) $460   _____

5) £2,500   _____

Language tip

To ask about currency rates you say *How many Euros to the dollar?*

Saying goodbye

6 **Two satisfied guests leave the Casablanca. Put their conversation with Susan in the correct order.**

(a) **Mr Smith**   I'm not sure …

    Susan   Here's one, it's always better to book your table in advance.

    Mrs Smith   Thank you very much.

    Susan   Could I get your coats?

(b) **Mr Smith**   Thank you. Goodbye.

    Susan   Goodbye.

(c) **Mr Smith**   Yes, please.

    Mrs Smith   It's a light brown raincoat and a grey coat.

    Susan   Here they are. Let me help you madam.

    Mrs Smith   Thank you very much.

    Susan   We look forward to seeing you again.

(d) **Susan**   Was everything to your satisfaction?

    Mrs Smith   Yes, everything was perfect.

    Mr Smith   We'll certainly come back soon.

    Susan   Do you have our card?

🎧 **Now listen and check your answers.**

Speechwork

7 **Susan gives Jan some advice on saying goodbye to guests. Match the tips to phrases in the conversation above. Then practise saying the phrases politely.**

1) check the guests are satisfied

2) offer the restaurant's card

3) get the guests' coats

4) help them put their coats on

5) say we hope to see them again

6) say goodbye

8 **Work in pairs. Use the information to write a dialogue. Practise your dialogue and then read it to the class.**

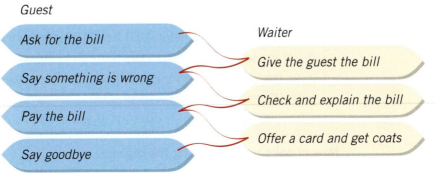

Guest

Ask for the bill

Say something is wrong

Pay the bill

Say goodbye

Waiter

Give the guest the bill

Check and explain the bill

Offer a card and get coats

1 Complete the sentences with the correct form of the past simple.

Liam Neil, yesterday I (*ask*) ....asked....... 1 you to clean the fridge. (*you / do*)
..........................2 it?

Neil Well, I (*be*) ....3 very busy: first I (*make*) ....4 a sauce, then
I (*put*) ....5 the rolls in the oven and finally I (*go*) ....6 to the
dining-room and I (*bring*) ....7 all the dishes to the kitchen. When I
(*finish*) ....8 I (*clean*) ....9 the oven, but I
(*not / clean*) ....10 the fridge.

2 Complete the sentences with the correct form of the present perfect.

Neil I (*clean*) ...'ve cleaned... 1 the fridge. Also, I (*wash*) ....2 the dirty dishes,
I (*help*) ....3 the fish cook, and I (*prepare*) ....4 the salads.

Liam And (*you / grate*) ....5 the carrots?

Neil No, I (*not / grate*) ....6 the carrots yet. I'll do that right away.

3 Complete the sentences with the correct options.

1 I've served *much / a lot of* Italian tourists today.
2 Would you like to have *a lot of / many* money?
3 I haven't got *many / much* time.
4 Have you prepared *many / much* fruit salad for tonight?
5 I usually have *a lot of / much* sugar in my coffee.
6 I've visited *much / a lot of* bars in New York.

4 Put the sentences in the correct order to complete the dialogue.

☐ a) These are the house speciality. They're made of mashed vegetables and chicken
coated with breadcrumbs and deep-fried. They're served with a salad.

☐ b) Certainly, sir. Thank you.

☐ c) Well, could you tell me what paella is?

[1] d) Are you ready to order, sir?

☐ e) Excellent choice, sir. And what would you like as a starter?

☐ f) Yes, good idea. I'll have a glass of that.

☐ g) Good. I'll try those.

☐ h) It sounds delicious. I think I'll have that as a main course.

☐ i) Let me see ... What exactly are Granny's croquettes?

☐ j) So the croquettes and then the paella. And what would you like to drink? Can I
recommend our sparkling white wine?

☐ k) It's a traditional Spanish rice dish. If you like seafood, I suggest you try it.

Now in pairs practise saying the dialogue.

5 Choose the correct option in the following situations.

1 A guest complains that there's a mistake on his bill: four times twenty makes eighty, not 100. What do you say?
   a) I'm afraid that twenty multiplied by four makes 100, sir.
   b) You're absolutely right, sir. Please accept my apologies.
   c) Let me see what I can do about it, sir.

2 A guest complains that the wine is corked. What do you say?
   a) I do apologise, sir. Let me clean it for you.
   b) I'll see to it personally that you're served as soon as possible.
   c) I'm very sorry, sir. I'll bring another bottle right away.

3 Two guests are leaving the restaurant. What do you say?
   a) We look forward to seeing you again.
   b) We'll certainly come back soon.
   c) Everything was to your satisfaction.

4 A guest says that she wants to pay by credit card. What do you say?
   a) Very well, madam. Here's your receipt and your tip.
   b) Certainly, madam. We accept Visa, American Express and MasterCard.
   c) I'm afraid we accept Visa, American Express and MasterCard.

6 Use the clues below to complete the crossword.

Across ▶

3 A cold dessert, delicious in summer. (3, 5 letters)
5 Starter: thin slices of raw fish or meat. (9 letters)
8 Not enough personnel. Word used as an excuse. (12 letters)
10 Complaint: the meat is not tender. (5 letters)

Down ▼

1 A traditional French dessert: it's flat and circular. (5 letters)
2 Something with a handle used to boil water. (8 letters)
4 Complaint about wine. (6 letters)
6 Method of payment: coins and bank notes. (4 letters)
7 Utensil used to grate food. (6 letters)
9 A hot, liquid starter. (4 letters)

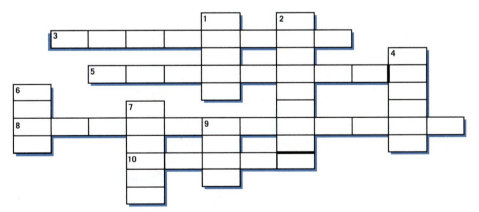

7 Work in pairs. Make short dialogues with these situations.

1 A guest complains about the food.
2 A guest complains about the service.
3 A guest wants to pay the bill and needs some clarification.
4 A guest is leaving the restaurant.

Pairwork

Unit 2 The workplace, ex 8 – Student A

Find five differences between your picture and your partner's.

In my picture there is / are ...
There isn't a / any ... in my picture.

Is there a ... in your picture?
Where is the ... in your picture?

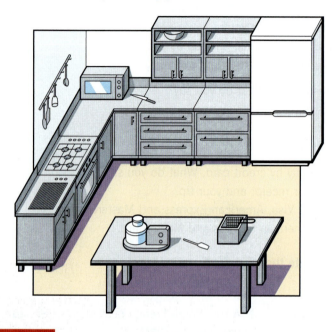

Unit 3 An enquiry, ex 6 – Student A

Describe this seating arrangement to your partner. Then draw a picture of the seating arrangement your partner describes to you.

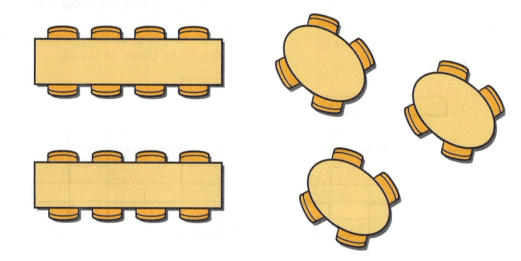

Unit 3 An enquiry, ex 7 – Student A

- Mr Collins is sitting next to Mr Thorpe.
- Mr Spencer is eating paella.
- Mrs Jones is eating a salad.

Pairwork

Unit 3 An enquiry, ex 7 – Student B

- Mrs Edwards is sitting opposite Mr Spencer.
- Mrs Robinson is sitting next to Mr Spencer.
- Mr Collins is eating a steak.
- Mrs Clark is eating duck.

Unit 11 Making a complaint, ex 7 – Student B

Find out from your partner which of the following jobs Jan has done. Then look at the picture below and answer your partner's questions.

- open windows
- change tablecloths
- empty ashtrays
- put out fresh flowers
- clear away dirty plates
- put out clean glasses

Pairwork

Pairwork

Unit 2 The workplace, ex 8 – Student B

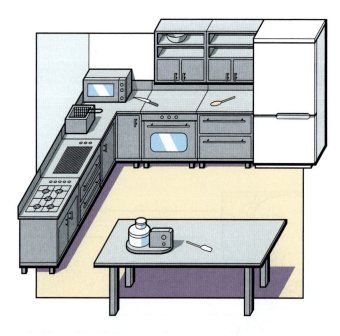

Unit 3 An enquiry, ex 6 – Student B

Describe this seating arrangement to your partner. Then draw a picture of the seating arrangement your partner describes to you.

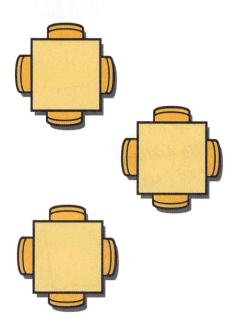

Pairwork

Unit 9 The menu, ex 8 – Student A

Use the verbs in the box to find out what your partner did last week.

serve	dance	practise your English	listen to music	talk	read

A: *Did you serve any guests last week?*   B: *Yes, I served lots of guests.*

Unit 3 An enquiry, ex 7 – Student C

* Mrs Jones is sitting at the small table with Mr Jones.
* Mr Thorpe is eating fish and chips.
* Mrs Edwards is eating pasta.

Unit 3 Giving directions, ex 7 – Student A

Ask your partner for directions to the following places. Mark them on the map.

* The Boudin Sourdough Bakery Coffee Shop next to the bakery in Jefferson Street.
* The Bay View Restaurant on Pier 39.
* The Fisherman's and Seaman's Chapel.
* The Cannery in Jefferson Street.

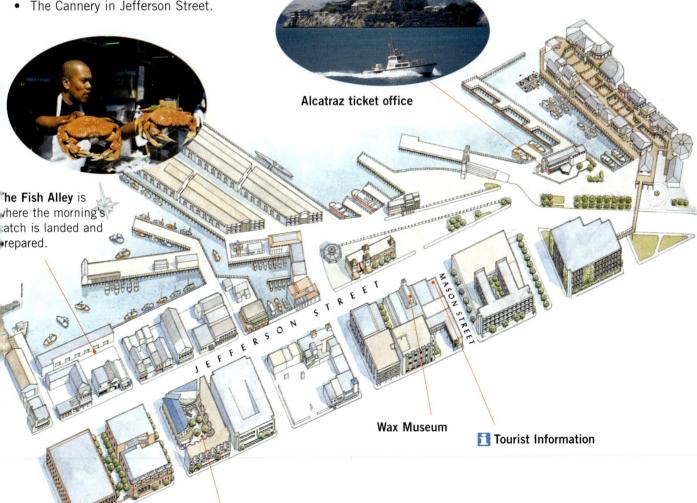

Alcatraz ticket office

The Fish Alley is where the morning's catch is landed and prepared.

Wax Museum

ℹ Tourist Information

The Anchorage shopping center

Pairwork

Unit 2 First day at work, ex 6 – Student A

Make questions with the following information.

| like wine | work in a restaurant | have a mobile telephone | read magazines |
| live in a city | listen to music a lot | work weekends | |

A: Do you like wine?
B: Yes, I do / No, I don't.

A: She likes / doesn't like wine.

Unit 4 Taking reservations, ex 8 – Student A

Look at the clocks below. Tell your partner the time and write down the times your partner tells you.

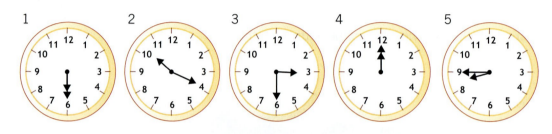

1   2   3   4   5

Unit 3 An enquiry, ex 7 – Student D

- Mr Thorpe is sitting back to back with Mrs Jones.
- Mrs Clark is sitting opposite Mr Thorpe.
- Mrs Robinson is eating a pizza.
- Mr Jones is eating a hamburger.

Conversion tables

WEIGHT

Imperial	Metric
1 oz	25 g
2 oz	55 g
3 1/2 oz	100 g
5 1/2 oz	150 g
1 lb	450 g
1 lb 2 oz	500 g
2 lb 4 oz	1 kg
3 lb 5 oz	1.5 kg
4 lb 8 oz	2 kg
6 lb 8 oz	3 kg

VOLUME

Imperial	Metric
1/4 tsp	1.25 ml
1/2 tsp	2.5 ml
1 tsp	5 ml
2 tsp	10 ml
3 tsp / 1 tbsp	15 ml
2 tbsp	30 ml
3 tbsp	45 ml
4 tbsp	60 ml
5 tbsp	75 ml
6 tbsp	90 ml

AMERICAN CUPS

Cups	Metric
1/4 cup	60 ml
1/3 cup	70 ml
1/2 cup	125 ml
2/3 cup	150 ml
3/4 cup	175 ml
1 cup	250 ml
1 1/2 cups	375 ml
2 cups	500 ml
3 cups	750 ml
4 cups	1 litre
6 cups	1.5 litres

TEMPERATURE

°C	°F
70	150
80	175
100	200
110	225
130	250
140	275
150	300
170	325
180	350
190	375
200	400
220	425
230	450
240	475
250	500
270	525
290	550

ABBREVIATIONS

tsp	teaspoon
tbsp	tablespoon
oz	ounce
fl oz	fluid ounce
lb	pound
g / gr	gram
kg	kilogram
l	litre
cl	centilitre
ml	millilitre

Grammar reference

Unit 1

The verb *be*

Positive

subject	verb
I	am
you / we / they	are
he / she / it	is

Negative

subject	verb	not
I	am	
you / we / they	are	not
he / she / it	is	

Question

verb	subject
am	I ?
are	you / we / they ?
Is	he / she / it ?

Short forms

I am	→	I'm	→	I'm not
You are	→	you're	→	you aren't
He is	→	he's	→	he isn't

Unit 2

Present simple

Positive

subject	verb
I / you / we / they	drink
he / she / it	drinks

Negative

subject	do	not	verb
I / you / we / they	do	not	drink
he / she / it	does		drink

Question

do	subject	verb
do	I / you / we / they	drink?
does	he / she / it	drink?

Short forms

I / you / we / they	→	don't
He / she / it	→	doesn't

▶ Use

We use the present simple to talk about:

– repeated actions

He always arrives late.

– permanent states

I live in London.

Note!

We add -*s* to the verb after *he* / *she* / *it*.

Grammar reference

There is / There are

Positive

There	be	object
there	is	a free table
	are	free tables

Question

Be	there	object
is	there	a free table?
are		free tables?

Negative

There	be / not	object
there	isn't	a free table
	aren't	any free tables

▶ Use

• We use *there is* with:

– countable nouns

There is a dirty cup on the table.

– uncountable nouns

There is some milk in the fridge.

• We use *there are* with countable nouns

*There are two kilos of tomatoes left.*x

Note!

For more detailed information on countable and uncountable nouns see page 96.

Unit 3

Present continuous

Positive

subject	verb	-ing form
I	am	
you / we / they	are	serving
he / she / it	is	

Question

Be	subject	-ing form
am	I	
are	you / we / they	serving?
Is	he / she / it	

Negative

subject	be	not	verb
I	am		
you / we / they	are	not	serving
he / she / it	is		

Short forms

am not	→	'm not
is not	→	isn't
are not	→	aren't

▶ Use

We use the present continuous to talk about what's happening now.

I am working at the moment.

Grammar reference

Unit 4

Prepositions of time

▶ Use

- We use *in* with parts of the day, months and seasons.
  *I'm sorry madam, but the restaurant closes **in** the evening.*
  *Special prices for Christmas banquets **in** December.*
  *Closed **in** winter.*

- We use *at* with times.
  *A table for two **at** seven o'clock this evening.*

- We use *on* with days.
  *All right, so that's a table for two **on** Saturday.*

- We use *from ... to ...* to show the beginning and end of something.
  *Traditional English breakfast available **from** 7 **to** 10 a.m.*

Unit 5

Modal verbs

Positive

subject	modal	verb
	can	
I	could	
you	will	
he / she / it	would	cook?
we	may	
they	shall	
	might	

Negative

subject	modal	*not*	verb
	cannot		
I	could		
you	will		
he / she / it	would	not	cook
we	may		
they	shall		
	might		

Question

modal	subject	verb
Can		
Could	I	
Will	you	
Would	he / she / it	cook?
May	we	
Shall	they	
Might		

Short forms

cannot	→	can't
could not	→	couldn't
will not	→	won't
would not	→	wouldn't
shall not	→	shan't

Grammar reference

▶ Use

- We use *can* to talk about:
  - ability
  I went to school and now I can make a perfect soufflé.
  - possibility
  I think I can bake the rolls while I prepare the muffins.

- We use *could*:
  - as the past of *can*
  When I was young I could work faster than I can now.
  - to make polite requests
  Could you bring me some more bread, please?

- We use *will* to talk about decisions taken at the moment of speaking:
  I think I'll take the roast beef.

- We use *would* to ask questions politely:
  Would you like some more tea, madam?

- We use *may* to:
  - ask permission
  May I smoke here?
  - express likelihood
  I may try the bamboo, it sounds very exotic.

- We use *shall* to make polite offers:
  Shall I close the window for you, sir?

Note!

Modal verbs never add -s to *he / she / it.*
The soufflé will̶s̶ be ready in a minute.

Going to + verb

Positive

subject	be	going to	verb
I	am		
he / she / it	is	going to	try
you / we / they	are		

Negative

subject	be	not	going to	verb
I	am			
he / she / it	is	not	going to	try
you / we / they	are			

Question

subject	be	going to	verb
am	I		
is	he / she / it	going to	try?
are	you / we / they		

Short forms

am not going to ...	→	'm not going to ...
is not going to ...	→	isn't going to ...
are not going to ...	→	aren't going to ...

▶ Use

We use *going to* + verb to talk about plans.
***I'm going to set** twenty-five dinner plates.*

Grammar reference

Unit 6

Countable and uncountable nouns

▶ Use

- Countable nouns can be singular or plural and they can have *a / an* or a number.
  *There is **an** egg on the table.*
  *There are **three** eggs behind the bar.*

- Uncountable nouns are never plural and cannot have *a / an* or a number.
  There is sugar behind the bar.

Note!

Both countable and uncountable nouns can use *some / any.*

Some / any

▶ Use

- *Some* is used with positive countable and uncountable verbs.
  *There are **some** new workers at the Casablanca.*
  *There is **some** sugar in the bowl.*

- *Any* is used with negative countable and uncountable verbs and questions.
  *There aren't **any** glasses on the tray.*
  *There isn't **any** milk.*
  *Is there **any** sauce left?*
  *Are there **any** clean glasses?*

Unit 7

Imperatives

- Imperatives do not have a subject before the verb.
  ***Add** grenadine and a splash of soda water.*

- To make negative instructions we place *don't* (never *doesn't*) before the verb:
  ***Don't** worry, you can have the recipe.*

▶ Use

Imperatives are sentences we use to give instructions.
***Serve** the dessert when it's ready.*

Unit 8

Comparatives and superlatives

Regular forms

	comparative form	superlative form
short adjectives	*colder* + **than**	**the** + *coldest*
adjectives ending in *-y*	*friendlier* + **than**	**the** + *friendliest*
long adjectives	**more** + *expensive* + **than**	**the** + **most** + *expensive*

Grammar reference

Irregular forms

adjective	comparative form	superlative form
good	better	the best
bad	worse	the worst

Transforming a verb into an adjective

To say how an ingredient is prepared, add *-ed* to the verb of preparation.

slice → *slic**ed***

gratinate → *gratinat**ed***

Because they are adjectives, they will appear before the ingredient.

sliced beef
gratinated macaroni

Unit 9

Past simple (regular verbs)

Positive

subject	verb	object
I / you / he / she / it / we / they	prepared	dinner

Negative

subject	*did*	*not*	verb	object
I / you / he / she / it / we / they	did	not	prepare	dinner

Question

Did	subject	verb	object
did	I / you / he / she / it / we / they	prepare	dinner?

Short forms

did + not	→	didn't

Unit 10

Past simple: *was / were*

Positive

subject	*be*
I / he / she / it	was
you / we / they	were

Negative

Subject	*be*	not
I / he / she / it	was	not
you / we / they	were	not

Question

Be	subject
was	I / he / she / it?
were	you / we / they?

Short forms

was + not	→	wasn't
were + not	→	weren't

Grammar reference

Note!

Never use *did* with the verb *be*.
She ~~didn't be~~ very busy yesterday.

Past simple (irregular verbs)

Positive

subject	verb	object
I / you / he / she / it / we / they	drank	wine

Negative

subject	*did*	*not*	verb	object
I / you / he / she / it / we / they	did	not	drink	wine

Question

Did	subject	verb	object
did	I / you / he / she it / we / they	drink	wine?

▶ **Use**

We use the past simple to talk about past actions.

Karl **baked** the cakes a little too early.
Peter **made** her a cocktail.
We **didn't prepare** enough salad servings yesterday.

Note!

We use the infinitive form of the verb in negatives and questions.

Unit 11

Present perfect

Positive

subject	*have*	-ed form	object
I / you / we / they	have	washed	the dishes
he / she / it	has	washed	the dishes

Negative

subject	*have*	*not*	-ed form	object
I / you / we / they	have	not	washed	the dishes
he / she / it	has	not	washed	the dishes

Question

have	subject	-ed form	object
have	I / you we / they	washed	the dishes?
has	he / she / it	washed	the dishes?

Short forms

have not	→	haven't
has not	→	hasn't

Grammar reference

▶ Use

We use the present perfect to talk about things we have done or made.
*I ordered the scallops and you've **brought** the sole!*

Note!

Remember that in the case of irregular verbs, you must use the third-column form of the list below.

Unit 12

Much / many / a lot of

	positive	negative	questions
countable nouns	a lot	many	many
uncountable nouns	a lot	much	much

▶ Use

We use *much / many / a lot of* to talk about quantities.
*There's **a lot of** ice cream in the fridge.*
*There aren't **many** starters on the menu.*
*I don't want **much** ice in my drink.*

Irregular verbs

INFINITIVE	PAST SIMPLE	PAST PARTICIPLE	INFINITIVE	PAST SIMPLE	PAST PARTICIPLE
become	became	become	have	had	had
be	was / were	been	hear	heard	heard
begin	began	begun	keep	kept	kept
bite	bit	bitten	know	knew	known
break	broke	broken	leave	left	left
bring	brought	brought	make	made	made
burn	burnt (or burned)	burnt (or burned)	meet	met	met
buy	bought	bought	pay	paid	paid
choose	chose	chosen	put	put	put
come	came	come	read /riːd/	read /red/	read /red/
cost	cost	cost	shake	shook	shaken
cut	cut	cut	spend	spent	spent
do	did	done	spill	spilt (or spilled)	spilt (or spilled)
drink	drank	drunk	spread	spread	spread
eat	ate	eaten	stand	stood	stood
find	found	found	take	took	taken
forget	forgot	forgotten	tell	told	told
freeze	froze	frozen	think	thought	thought
get	got	got	understand	understood	understood
give	gave	given	write	wrote	written
go	went	gone			

Tapescripts

Tapescripts

UNIT 1 MEET THE BOSS, EX 10

1 0034 93 766544
2 0044 288 8467771
3 001 262 567381
4 0048 22 773155
5 0033 33 54038
6 0030 1 337 3170

UNIT 1 MEET THE BOSS, EX 11

1   Could you take this to room 11?
2   Your room number is 28.
3   Where is room 18?
4   This is the key card for room 25.
5   This is the safety box for room 30.
6   Room 3 is very quiet.
7   Mr Smith is in room 21.
8   Is room 8 a double room?
9   The TV in room 5 doesn't work.
10 Is room 13 near the emergency exit?
11 A bottle of champagne for room 23, please.
12 The people in room 14 leave tomorrow.

UNIT 2 FIRST DAY AT WORK, EX 3

1 a) Do you speak <u>Spanish</u>?
   b) Do <u>you</u> speak Spanish?
2 a) Is <u>Sam</u> here?
   b) Is Sam <u>here</u>?
3 a) He always arrives <u>late</u>.
   b) He <u>always</u> arrives late.
4 a) I <u>don't</u> drink coffee.
   b) I don't drink <u>coffee</u>.
5 a) These are the <u>toilets</u>.
   b) <u>These</u> are the toilets.
6 a) The dining-room's on the <u>right</u>.
   b) The <u>dining-room's</u> on the right.

UNIT 2 THE WORKPLACE, EX 4

1 She's responsible for the kitchen.
2 I prepare the sauces.
3 He's in charge of the bar area.
4 He serves the guests in the dining-room.
5 She assists the cooks.

UNIT 2 THE WORKPLACE, EX 7

1 There are two new workers at the Casablanca.
2 There's an oven in the pastry section.
3 There <u>isn't</u> a fridge in the meat section.
4 There are three objects on the table.
5 There <u>aren't</u> any guests in the bar.

UNIT 3 AN ENQUIRY, EX 4

1 <u>What</u> do you do?
2 <u>Who</u> is that man?
3 <u>Where</u> is the toilet?
4 <u>When</u> do you open?
5 <u>How</u> are you?
6 <u>Why</u> are you nervous?

UNIT 3 AN ENQUIRY, EX 5

Jan   Excuse me Ms Davies, I think there's a problem with the tables for the wedding banquet. There are only four medium-sized tables in the restaurant. We can seat five guests at each table, but there are twenty-five guests. So we need one more but the rest of the tables are square or rectangular.

Susan   Well, why don't we arrange the tables in a U-shape and not banqueting style? I'll phone Ms Porter and check it's OK.

UNIT 4 TAKING RESERVATIONS, EX 4

Call 1

Jan   Good afternoon, the Casablanca Restaurant. Can I help you?
Mrs Kerrigan   Yes, I would like to make a reservation.
Jan   Certainly madam. When is it for?
Mrs Kerrigan   Saturday.
Jan   And what time would you like?
Mrs Kerrigan   Eleven o'clock in the evening, please.
Jan   I'm sorry madam but the restaurant closes at eleven o'clock.
Mrs Kerrigan   Oh, is ten o'clock OK?
Jan   Certainly madam. And how many people is it for?
Mrs Kerrigan   For two.
Jan   OK. Can I have your name, please?
Mrs Kerrigan   Mrs Kerrigan.
Jan   Could you spell that, please?
Mrs Kerrigan   Yes, it's K-E-double R-I-G-A-N.
Jan   So, that's a table for two at ten o'clock on Saturday.

Mrs Kerrigan	Thanks very much. Bye.
Jan	Thanks for calling. Bye.

Call 2

Jan	Good evening, the Casablanca Restaurant. Can I help you?
Mrs Fox	I'd like to book a table for four on Sunday evening.
Jan	Very well madam. What time would you like?
Mrs Fox	At about eight o'clock. Is that OK?
Jan	Certainly madam. What's the name, please?
Mrs Fox	It's Fox.
Jan	OK, so that's a table for four at eight o'clock on Sunday. Thank you very much Mrs Fox.
Caller	Thank you. Goodbye.

UNIT 4 TAKING RESERVATIONS, EX 7

1 We open at twelve o'clock midday.
2 A table for two at half past three, please.
3 Last orders are at a quarter to eleven.
4 I get to work at about ten to nine.
5 We open at two, after lunch.
6 We close at half eleven in the evening.
7 There's a table free at a quarter to four.
8 I got home at five forty-five in the morning!

UNIT 4 THE CASABLANCA RESTAURANT, EX 4

1 So, that's a table for six on Tuesday 18 March.
2 I started work at the Casablanca in April.
3 The wedding's on Wednesday 2 June.
4 We're open till midnight on Saturday 24 December.
5 I came to London in May this year.
6 The restaurant opened on Friday 20 August.

UNIT 5 RECEIVING GUESTS, EX 4

Dialogue 1

A: So, where are we going to seat Mr and Mrs Jones tonight?
B: What about the small square table near the window?
A: All right.

Dialogue 2

A: And where would you like to sit?
B: Is there a round table for twelve in the
   non-smoking section?
A: I'm sorry, madam, but there are no large round tables.

Dialogue 3

A: Look at that woman! What a lovely dress!
B: Where?
A: Over there, on the terrace.
B: At the oval table?
A: Yes. That's her.

UNIT 5 A WEDDING BANQUET, EX 6

There's a dish on the tray. On the right of the dish there's a knife and on the left of the dish there's a napkin. The spoon is in the middle of the tray, near the dish. On the right of the spoon there's a saucer and there's a cup on the saucer. On the left of the tray there are a milk jug, a teapot and a sugar bowl. The teapot is between the milk jug and the sugar bowl. The sugar bowl is on the right of the teapot.

UNIT 6 THE DRINKS MENU, EX 5

1 A hot black coffee with whisky, sugar and cream.
2 A cocktail made of cola, rum and lime juice.
3 An expensive French sparkling wine.
4 An Italian drink made with espresso coffee and cream.
5 A type of beer that is very popular in Britain.
6 An alcoholic drink from Scotland or Ireland.

UNIT 7 MAKING COCKTAILS, EX 8

1 First / mix the mint leaves.
2 I really like it / what is it?
3 Then / add the ice.
4 Relax / and let me prepare you a drink.
5 I'm afraid it's not Spanish / it's Cuban.
6 Finally / stir and garnish with lime zest.

UNIT 8 A SEAFOOD RECIPE, EX 5

/ɪd/
gratinated, grated, marinated
/d/ or /t/
cooked, poured, picked, sliced, fried, mashed, covered, sprinkled, buttered

UNIT 9 PRONOUNCING FRENCH WORDS, EX 4

1 pâté	2 vichyssoise	3 mornay	4 meunière
5 croquette	6 sommelier	7 sautéed	8 rosé

UNIT 10 A DESSERT RECIPE, EX 7

1 I'm on a diet. I'd like something light as a dessert. What can you recommend?
2 It's very hot. I feel like a cold dessert. What do you suggest?
3 I'd like some ice cream but I don't like nuts. Do you have any fruit flavours?
4 I don't want anything sweet. What other desserts do you have?

5 I would like something refreshing. What would you recommend?

6 Ice cream sounds good but nothing with caffeine in it please.

UNIT 11 MAKING A COMPLAINT, EX 2

Dialogue 1
Guest   Waiter, please!
Waiter   Yes, sir. How can I help you?
Guest   I think there's been a mistake. I ordered the scallops and you've brought the sole!
Waiter   I'm very sorry sir. I'll change it for you.

Dialogue 2
Guest   Waiter, this soup is too salty!
Waiter   I'm sorry madam. Would you like to order something else?
Guest   Well, yes. Can I have another look at the menu, please?
Waiter   Certainly madam. I'll bring it straightaway.

Dialogue 3
Guest   Waiter, this wine has a strange taste. I think it's corked.
Susan   I'm very sorry, madam. I'll bring you another bottle immediately.
Guest   Thank you.

Dialogue 4
Waiter   Is everything to your satisfaction?
Guest   Actually, I find the steak too rare for my taste.
Waiter   I'll ask the chef to put it back on the grill.
Guest   That's great. Thanks.

Dialogue 5
Guest   Excuse me, this piece of chocolate cake has marmalade in it. Would it be possible to have another one without it?
Susan   I'm afraid it won't be possible madam. There's marmalade on the whole cake.
Guest   Oh, I really don't like marmalade.
Susan   Would you like to order something else? Can I suggest the chocolate mousse or the brownie?

UNIT 11 DEALING WITH COMPLAINTS, EX 3

Ask what the problem is
d) What is the problem?
Apologise
a) Please accept my apologies.
b) I do apologise sir.
i) I'm very sorry sir.
Explain the reason for the problem

e) There aren't any more tables available.
g) I'm afraid we're very busy this evening.
Offer a solution or compensation
c) I'll go and ask the manager to come.
f) I'll ask the chef to heat it up for you.
h) Could we offer you a coffee on the house?
j) We'll pay for it to be cleaned.

UNIT 11 DEALING WITH COMPLAINTS, EX 4

Guest   Waiter!
Waiter   Yes madam. How can I help you?
Guest   We ordered our food forty minutes ago.
Waiter   I apologise, madam. I'm afraid we're very busy and we're short-staffed. I'll see to it personally that you're served as soon as possible.
Guest   We'd appreciate that. Thank you. And, another thing, this glass is dirty. There's lipstick on it!
Waiter   I'm terribly sorry madam. I'll bring a clean one immediately.
Guest   Thank you.

UNIT 11 DEALING WITH COMPLAINTS, EX 5

1 We ordered sparkling water, not still. (US)
2 This tomato soup is cold. (US)
3 We can't dance here. The music is awful! (UK)
4 Could we have another bottle of wine? This one's corked. (US)
5 I'm afraid we can't seat forty people madam. (UK)
6 The waiter isn't very friendly, is he? (UK)
7 We can't talk here – the music's too loud. (US)
8 We ordered our food over half an hour ago. (UK)

UNIT 12 ASKING FOR THE BILL, EX 2

Dialogue 1
Guest   Can I have the bill, please?
Waiter   Certainly madam. Just a moment please. Here you are madam.
Guest   Thank you. Can I pay by credit card?
Waiter   We accept Visa, American Express and MasterCard.
Guest   Perfect I'll pay by Visa.
Waiter   Very well madam. Will you sign here, please?
Guest   Yes, of course.
Waiter   Here's your bill and your receipt madam.
Guest   Thank you.

Dialogue 2
Guest 1 Could you bring us the bill, please?
Waiter   Yes, sir. I'll bring it immediately.
Guest 2 Can we pay by traveller's cheque?

Waiter	I'm afraid we don't accept traveller's cheques sir.
Guest 2	OK. Can we pay in US dollars?
Waiter	Yes, sir. I'll ask the cashier to prepare the bill in dollars. Here you are sir.
Guest 1	Is service included in the bill?
Waiter	Yes, sir, it is.
Guest 2	Let's leave him a tip anyway John, the service was excellent.

Dialogue 3

Guest:	How much is it?
Bartender	One moment sir. I'll prepare the bill. Here you are sir. The bill.
Guest	Oh, that's a lot of money! Is tax included?
Bartender	Yes, sir. VAT is automatically charged.
Guest	I see.
Bartender	How will you be paying, sir? In cash or by credit card?
Guest	In cash and keep the change.
Bartender	Thank you, sir.

UNIT 12 EXPLAINING THE BILL, EX 1

Pedro	Waiter!
Jan	Can I help you, sir?
Pedro	Yes. We'd like to check the bill. You see, we ordered three table d'hôte menus, at £20 each. Three times twenty makes £60. So how does the bill come to £121.61?
Jan	Let me see sir. I think you ordered three apéritifs, wine and two spirits too.
Mrs Gracia	Isn't this all included in the table d'hôte menu?
Jan	I'm afraid it isn't madam. You see, here it says 'Drinks not included.'
Pedro	But that still doesn't make £121.61.
Jan	You also have to add the VAT plus the service to the £92 sir.
Mr Gracia	Do you do family discounts?
Jan	I'm sorry sir?
Mr Gracia	You see our daughter, Rosa, works here.
Jan	Rosa?
Pedro	So, could you tell her her parents and her boyfriend are here, please?
Jan	Boyfriend? Er …
Mr Gracia	Are you OK?
Jan	Yes, yes. I'll go and tell Rosa.
Rosa	Mama! Papa! Pedro!
All	Rosa!

UNIT 12 EXPLAINING THE BILL, EX 4

1   One hundred and eight plus two point five equals one hundred and ten point five.

2   One thousand six hundred minus two hundred and four equals one thousand three hundred and ninety-six.

3   Four hundred and forty-seven multiplied by two equals eight hundred and ninety-four.

4   Five hundred and fifty plus sixty-three equals six hundred and thirteen.

5   Sixty-nine divided by three equals twenty-three.

6   Seven hundred and fifty-seven minus eighty-nine equals six hundred and sixty-eight.

7   Five times nineteen equals ninety-five.

8   Nine thousand nine hundred and ninety-nine plus one equals ten thousand.

9   Two and a half plus one hundred and seven equals one hundred and nine and a half.

10   Seven point three five minus one point two one equals six point one four.

UNIT 12 EXPLAINING THE BILL, EX 6

Susan	Was everything to your satisfaction?
Mrs Smith	Yes, everything was perfect.
Mr Smith	We'll certainly come back soon.
Susan	Do you have our card?
Mr Smith	I'm not sure.
Susan	Here's one, it's always better to book your table in advance.
Mrs Smith	Thank you very much.
Susan	Could I get your coats?
Mr Smith	Yes, please.
Mrs Smith	It's a light brown raincoat and a grey coat.
Susan	Here they are. Let me help you madam.
Mrs Smith	Thank you very much.
Susan	We look forward to seeing you again.
Mr Smith	Thank you. Goodbye.
Susan	Goodbye.

Glossary

English	Your language	English	Your language

Appliances

blender ....
coffee-grinder ....
coffee machine / coffee maker ....
deep-fryer ....
dishwasher ....
electric kettle ....
extractor fan ....
food mixer ....
food processor ....
fridge ....
grill ....
microwave oven ....
oven ....
salamander grill ....
stove ....
walk-in freezer ....

Cereal products

bread ....
breadcrumbs ....
cereal ....
croissant ....
flour ....
oats ....
pastry ....
rice ....
roll ....
sandwich ....
semolina ....
toast ....

Complaints

bad ....
blunt ....
broken ....

busy ....
cold ....
corked ....
cracked ....
dirty ....
draughty ....
filthy ....
missing ....
noisy ....
overcooked ....
rude ....
salty ....
slow ....
spicy ....
stained ....
stale ....
tough ....
underdone ....
unfriendly ....
wrong ....

Dairy products

butter ....
cheese ....
cottage cheese ....
cream ....
egg ....
fried egg ....
goat's cheese ....
hard boiled egg ....
mascarpone ....
milk ....
omelette (UK) / omelet (US) ....
poached egg ....
scrambled egg ....
soft boiled egg ....

English	Your language	English	Your language

yoghurt ....

whipping cream ....

Describing food & drinks

bad ....

boiled ....

bottled ....

canned ....

cheap ....

chilled ....

creamy ....

crispy ....

draught ....

dry ....

expensive ....

good ....

grilled ....

herbal ....

jacket ....

medium ....

poor ....

popular ....

rare ....

rich ....

roast ....

sautéed ....

soft ....

sparkling ....

spongy ....

still ....

sweet ....

tasty ....

tinned ....

traditional ....

well-done ....

Describing restaurants

beautiful ....

characteristic ....

comfortable ....

cosy ....

exotic ....

famous ....

first-class ....

luxurious ....

modern ....

new ....

old ....

packed ....

spacious ....

traditional ....

Dishes

biscuit (UK) / cookie (US)

brownie ....

cake ....

carpaccio ....

caviare ....

couscous ....

crème caramel ....

croquette ....

fruit salad ....

ice cream ....

jelly ....

kebab ....

lasagne ....

mousse ....

paella ....

pancakes / crêpes ....

pasta ....

pâté ....

pie ....

Glossary

English	Your language	English	Your language

sorbet ....

stew ....

sushi ....

trifle ....

tzatziki ....

vichyssoise ....

Drinks (alcoholic)

ale ....

apéritif ....

beer ....

bitter ....

brandy ....

champagne ....

cocktail ....

cognac ....

Cuba Libre ....

gin ....

house wine ....

Irish coffee ....

lager ....

liqueur ....

long drink ....

on the rocks ....

port ....

sherry ....

soda ....

spirit (UK) / liquor (US) ....

vodka ....

whisky ....

(white, red, rosé) wine ....

Drinks (non-alcoholic)

camomile tea ....

cappuccino ....

cocoa / drinking chocolate ....

coffee ....

decaffeinated coffee ....

espresso ....

fruit juice / fruit squash ....

hot drink ....

lemonade ....

milk ....

milk shake ....

mineral water ....

plain water ....

pop / soda (US) ....

soft drink ....

tea ....

tonic ....

Fish

anchovy ....

angler / monkfish ....

cod ....

eel ....

hake ....

halibut ....

herring ....

mackerel ....

plaice ....

salmon ....

sardine ....

sole ....

trout ....

tuna ....

Fruit

apple ....

apricot ....

banana ....

cherry ....

English	Your language	English	Your language
grape	....	cinnamon	....
grapefruit	....	clove	....
kiwi	....	dill	....
lemon	....	mint leaf	....
lime	....	nutmeg	....
mandarin	....	parsley	....
melon	....	pepper	....
nut	....	rosemary	....
orange	....	saffron	....
peach	....	sage	....
pear	....	salt	....
pineapple	....	seasoning	....
plum	....	thyme	....
raspberry	....	vanilla	....
strawberry	....		
water-melon	....		
zest	....		

Furniture

English	Your language
chair	....
counter	....
cupboard	....
desk	....
high chair	....
rack	....
shelves	....
side table	....
sideboard	....
stool	....
table	....
trolley	....
worktop	....

Herbs and spices

English	Your language
bay leaf	
chilli (UK) / chili (US)	....

Jobs

English	Your language
bartender	....
cashier	....
chef / cook	....
chef de partie	....
chef de rang	....
commis	....
dining-room assistant	....
fish chef / cook	....
food and beverage manager	....
front waiter	....
garde manger	....
head chef	....
head waiter	....
kitchen assistant	....
maître d'hôtel	....
meat chef / cook	....
pastry chef / cook	....
reception waiter	....
restaurant manager	....
salad chef / cook	....

Glossary

English	Your language	English	Your language
sauce chef / cook		joint	
sommelier		lamb	
sous-chef / under-chef		meatball	
waiter		mincemeat	
wine waiter		mutton	
		pork	

Meals and menus

à la carte menu		poultry	
afternoon tea		rabbit	
breakfast		roast	
children's menu		sausage	
dinner		sirloin steak	
fish dish		steak	
high tea		steak tartare	
lunch		turkey	
main course		veal	
meat dish			

Methods of payment

side dish		banknote	
starter		bill (UK) / check (US)	
supper		business card	
table d'hôte menu		cash	
vegetarian dish		cheque (UK) / check (US)	
		coin	

Meat and poultry

		credit card	
bacon		guest	
beef		order form	
chicken		room key	
chop		traveller's cheque	
cold meat		signature	

Restaurant sections

cutlet			
duck		bar	
fillet steak (UK) / tenderloin (US)		car park (UK) / parking lot (US)	
goose		cloakroom	
ham		corner	
hamburger		dance floor	
horsemeat			

Glossary

English	Your language	English	Your language
dining-room	....	scampi	....
dishwashing section	....	shrimp	....
fish section	....	squid	....

English	Your language
garden	....
gents	....

Seating arrangements

English	Your language
ground floor	....
indoors	....
kitchen	....
ladies	....
lift (UK) / elevator (US)	....
lounge bar	....
meat section	....
non-smoking section	....
outdoors	....
pastry section	....
piano	....
private dining-room	....
reception	....
roof garden	....
sauce section	....
smoking section	....
storeroom	....
terrace	....
toilets	....
top floor	....
vegetable section	....
window	....

Seating arrangements:

English	Your language
banqueting style	....
conference style	....
horseshoe	....
large	....
medium-sized	....
oval	....
quiet	....
rectangular	....
round	....
shade	....
shape	....
size	....
small	....
square	....
sun	....
U-shape	....
view	....

Seafood

English	Your language
crayfish	....
lobster	....
mussel	....
octopus	....
oyster	....
prawn	....
scallop	....

Tableware

English	Your language
ashtray	....
bottle	....
bowl	....
cereal bowl	....
coaster	....
cocktail shaker	....
coffee pot	....
cork	....
cruet set	....
cup	....
decanter	....
dessertspoon	....

Glossary

English	Your language
dinner plate	....
fork	....
glass	....
ice bucket	....
knife	....
milk jug	....
mug	....
mustard pot	....
napkin	....
pepper grinder / pot	....
saltcellar	....
sauce boat / gravy boat	....
saucer	....
side plate	....
slipcloth	....
soup bowl	....
soup spoon	....
sugar bowl	....
tablecloth	....
tablespoon	....
tea-ball	....
teapot	....
teaspoon	....
tray	....
vase	....
whitecloth	....
wine basket	....
wine label	....

Utensils

baking tin	....
bottle-opener	....
casserole	....
chef's knife	....
colander	....
corkscrew	....
frying pan	....
grater	....
kettle	....
ladle	....
lid	....
mould	....
pan	....
potato peeler	....
saucepan	....
scissors	....
sieve	....
skimmer	....
spatula	....
strainer	....
tin-opener (UK) / can-opener (US)	....
wire whisk	....
wooden spoon	....

Vegetables

asparagus	....
aubergine (UK) / eggplant (US)	....
avocado pear	....
bean	....
beetroot	....
broccoli	....
Brussels sprout	....
cabbage	....
carrot	....
cauliflower	....
celery	....
chives	....
corn	....
courgette (UK) / zucchini (US)	....
cucumber	....
endive	....
garlic	....

English	Your language	English	Your language
leek	......	rim	......
lettuce	......	roast	......
mushroom	......	season	......
olive	......	shake	......
onion	......	simmer	......
pea	......	skim	......
pepper	......	slice	......
potato	......	sprinkle	......
spinach	......	stir	......
tomato	......	strain	......
		whip	......

Verbs of preparation

add	......
bake	......
beat	......
boil	......
butter	......
chop	......
combine	......
cook	......
cover	......
cut	......
drain	......
fill	......
fry	......
garnish	......
grate	......
grill (UK) / broil (US)	......
mash	......
melt	......
mix	......
muddle (US)	......
peel	......
pick	......
pour	......
refrigerate	......

Verbs (general)

apologise	......
arrive	......
attend	......
book	......
bring	......
check	......
cross	......
drink	......
go straight on	......
greet	......
leave	......
offer	......
pass	......
prepare	......
present	......
reserve	......
serve	......
show	......
speak	......
suggest	......
take	......
turn	......
walk	......